M000230288

Praise for *Different, Not Less*

'This book, like the author themselves, radiates a fierce, unapologetic and joyous Disability Pride that makes it impossible to put down. As a proud disabled person and someone who was a home-educated student themselves, chapter after chapter had me simultaneously whooping with joy and struggling to hold back tears. *Different, Not Less* is a glorious example of the Australian disability community moving into our power. This book is a marvel.'
JORDON STEELE-JOHN, DISABILITY RIGHTS ADVOCATE AND AUSTRALIAN SENATOR FOR WESTERN AUSTRALIA

'For too many years there have been books created by people who studied us, supported us or taught us. Finally, we are seeing a surge of autistic authors sharing their stories, and this is a truly shining example of why it makes such a difference. Chloé's heartfelt and powerful writing had me glued to my seat and turning the pages—which is no easy feat for this ADHD-er ... It will make you laugh, cry and snort out loud. It's hard to read, but Chloé always brings it back to sharing how we can make the world a better place for autistic girls. She safely brings us back to her glorious world of self-discovery and celebration only the way Chloé can, which reminds us why she is one of the most celebrated autistic advocates of our time.'
KATIE KOULLAS, CEO, YELLOW LADYBUGS

'Chloé's spirit in the face of adversity had me cheering! A powerful book packed with insights for building a future in which no one is left behind.'
TARYN BRUMFITT, FOUNDER OF THE BODY IMAGE MOVEMENT AND DIRECTOR OF *EMBRACE* AND *EMBRACE KIDS*

'Chloé Hayden has written the guide to life that I wish I'd been handed when I was an undiagnosed Autistic kid, unsure of my place in the world. Sparkling with the power of Autistic joy, this is a special book for neurodivergent young people, and for those who love and support them. Chloé's passionate advocacy is clear on every page—a book to change lives.'
CLEM BASTOW, AUTHOR OF *LATE BLOOMER*

APR 23

CHLOÉ HAYDEN

Different, Not Less

A neurodivergent's guide to embracing your true self and finding your happily ever after

murdoch books
Sydney | London

Published in 2022 by Murdoch Books, an imprint of Allen & Unwin

Copyright © Chloé Hayden 2022

All rights reserved. No part of this book may be reproduced or transmitted in any form or by any means, electronic or mechanical, including photocopying, recording or by any information storage and retrieval system, without prior permission in writing from the publisher. The Australian *Copyright Act 1968* (the Act) allows a maximum of one chapter or 10 per cent of this book, whichever is the greater, to be photocopied by any educational institution for its educational purposes provided that the educational institution (or body that administers it) has given a remuneration notice to the Copyright Agency (Australia) under the Act.

Murdoch Books Australia
83 Alexander Street, Crows Nest NSW 2065
Phone: +61 (0)2 8425 0100
murdochbooks.com.au
info@murdochbooks.com.au

Murdoch Books UK
Ormond House, 26–27 Boswell Street, London WC1N 3JZ
Phone: +44 (0) 20 8785 5995
murdochbooks.co.uk
info@murdochbooks.co.uk

A catalogue record for this book is available from the National Library of Australia

A catalogue record for this book is available from the British Library

ISBN 978 1 92261 618 0

Cover design by Amy Daoud
Text design by George Saad
Author photograph by Jayden Course

Typeset by Midland Typesetters
Printed and bound by CPI Group (UK) Ltd, Croydon, CR04YY

DISCLAIMER: The content presented in this book is meant for inspiration and informational purposes only. The author and publisher claim no responsibility to any person or entity for any liability, loss, or damage caused or alleged to be caused directly or indirectly as a result of the use, application, or interpretation of the material in this book.

Every reasonable effort has been made to trace the owners of copyright materials in this book, but in some instances this has proven impossible. The author(s) and publisher will be glad to receive information leading to more complete acknowledgements in subsequent printings of the book and in the meantime extend their apologies for any omissions.

The authors and publishers acknowledge that we meet and work on the traditional lands of the Cammeraygal, Gadigal and Wangal people of the Eora Nation and pay our respects to their elders past, present and future.

10 9 8

'Your life is an occasion. Rise to it.'

—*Mr. Magorium's Wonder Emporium*

Author's note

'Neurodiversity is:

- ★ *a state of nature to be respected*
- ★ *an analytical tool for examining social issues*
- ★ *an argument for the conservation and facilitation of human diversity.*

It is not *a synonym for "Neurological Disorder".'*

—Judy Singer, from her blog *Reflections on Neurodiversity*

Australian autistic sociologist Judy Singer first coined the term 'neurodiversity' in the late 1990s to describe the natural variation of brain function and behavioural differences that exist among humans, including conditions such as autism, ADHD, dyslexia and dyspraxia. Neurodiversity recognises that neurological differences are not inherently bad or problematic, but simply the result of variations in the human genome and our diverse human population.

INTRODUCTION

Once Upon a Time . . .

I've always been in love with the idea of fairytales, with a world of pastel colours, flower-covered fields, fairies and enchanting princesses, of magic and spontaneous music. A world in which the lead is considered a hero because of their differences, rather than ostracised and pushed aside for them, and where good and kind always overcome scary and evil. A world where 'happily ever afters' are a given, rather than a hopeful yearning.

Growing up, I wished desperately to be part of this world. I named all my soft toys after Disney characters, spoke almost solely in Disney quotes, hoarded fairytale memorabilia like a little goblin, blacked out as an eighteen year old when I met Tinkerbell at Disneyland and, for a good portion of my life, wore only clothing that I believed resembled my favourite fairytale princesses.

I looked to those princesses, fairies and anthropomorphised woodland creatures and pined with every fibre of my body to be like them, to have, as they did, a firm understanding of my place in the universe. Every night I left my bedroom window open on the off-chance Peter Pan would realise he'd forgotten a peculiar little girl, left her in the wrong universe, and come back, take her hand and whisk her away to a world of pirates, pixies and mermaids. Away from her own land, where life was as confusing and difficult as the hardest journey in any fairytale. Day after day, year after year, I sat, wishing, hoping, praying. But Peter didn't come.

My heart grew heavier as I slowly realised that life wasn't like fairytales. Perhaps magic was reserved only for princesses and knights in shining armour. Perhaps those shooting stars, upon which I had wished so hard, were just flaming balls of gas.

My teenage years were a tangle of emotions as I tried to forget the fantasy of a place where I fit in. Every part of my life, of society, of growing up reminded me again and again that fairytales were only for make-believe, and that happily ever afters didn't exist outside of storybooks. But my heart still deeply yearned for it, like a child at Disneyland who is 'too old' to believe in princesses but still feels their tummy twist in excitement when a princess waves to them, or who shuts their eyes just that little bit tighter on Christmas Eve so that Santa Clause will presume they're asleep and still leave them presents.

As I've gotten older, though, I've started to realise that perhaps my yearnings weren't unwarranted. Peter Pan may not be coming any time soon, and maybe I'm not going to look at my reflection in a pool of water and have all my hopes and dreams come true, but this isn't because fairytales aren't real. Not in the slightest. In fact, I believe in fairytales now more than ever. We are living them every day of our lives. Allow me to explain.

When we are introduced to fairytales, we learn that every single one of them has three fundamental stages, and my theory is that we can see these three stages in our own lives:

1. The **Once Upon a Time stage**, an introduction, an opening to a new adventure, the promise of something new. Fairytales need beginnings that aren't all sunflowers and butterflies—imagine if every fairytale started off with a happy protagonist backed by a joyful soundtrack and no evil lion uncles, sorcerers or poisoned apples in sight. Would that even be a story at all? Despite how much it may hurt, our Once Upon a Time needs to start somewhere challenging, maybe even a bit bleak, to launch us into our second stage.
2. The **Adventure stage** is about confronting dragons, great journeys and courageous battles. Your Adventure might not be with a fire-breathing beast, but perhaps it's with poor circumstances, ill mental health, a lack of accessibility and understanding, or a world of other challenges. Our Adventure

is where our stories begin to come together: we meet our sidekicks, we find the path to figure out who we are, and we begin to discover where our place is in the world.

3. And finally, if Disney has taught me anything, it's that if you think your fairytale is finished but you haven't reached your **Happily Ever After stage** yet, you are still only in the beginning chapters and you have many stages to go. A book cannot close without a Happily Ever After; a fairytale movie cannot end without a triumphant orchestral finale. And regardless of whatever happened during your Once Upon a Time and your Adventure stages, the same holds true for you: your Happily Ever After will come.

And the best part? Unlike traditional fairytales, in which every final page is exactly the same, *your* fairytale is not a closed book. You will experience many Once Upon a Times, Adventures and Happily Ever Afters. A Happily Ever After is not the end of your story, but merely the introduction to the next instalment.

I'll take any excuse to use a Disney analogy, and so throughout this book we're going to keep coming back to three Disney storylines that resonate especially strongly for me and that I believe beautifully depict these three stages: those of Genie in *Aladdin*, Quasimodo from *The Hunchback of Notre Dame* and Simba in *The Lion King*.

Maybe you haven't been trapped inside a magic lamp for thousands of years like Genie in *Aladdin*, but I know that many of us have felt just as trapped and scared as he did. Maybe you haven't been holed up in a bell tower in Paris like Quasimodo in *The Hunchback of Notre Dame*, but as society continues to tell us that we need to fit certain social norms and aesthetics in our appearance, identity, abilities and personalities, many of us have also felt like hiding away, thinking who we are is never going to be good enough. And maybe a crazed uncle didn't throw your father into a stampeding herd of wildebeest and blame the situation on you, as Simba's did in *The Lion King*, but I know there have been times in our lives when we've felt as betrayed, hurt and alone as Simba did.

The beginning of my own fairytale seemed picture-perfect. Much like Simba, I grew up in a safe, loving home where we never wanted for anything. I was surrounded by an amazing family and loving parents who always went above and beyond for me and my siblings. I had access to whatever I needed and my abilities and identity were never questioned or denied while I was surrounded by those who loved me. If you were to watch my Once Upon a Time, you might have assumed I was already at the Happily Ever After. But, despite what appeared to be the beginning of a charmed, easy story, I was the most terrified, scared, sad, worried little girl that you would ever meet.

I knew from a young age that my mind, my identity and who I was weren't wanted or valued in the wider community, that I wasn't what I was supposed to be.

In my fairytale, I was the trapped Genie.

In my fairytale, I was the hidden, misunderstood Quasimodo.

In my fairytale, I was the outcast that society had abandoned.

In my fairytale, I was Simba, the broken lion club.

I wasn't off to a good start.

Like all fairytales, the story you are about to read is one of overcoming difficulties, finding resilience, discovering a Happily Ever After and creating a life that is your own. We'll be exploring neurodiversity, autism, disability and mental health in a way that is still unspoken about in our society—a society that hasn't yet realised just how brilliant and needed different minds are. What's unusual here is that this book was written by a neurodivergent, disabled person—not by someone who has studied these topics from a distance, but by someone who lives them.

It's important to note that while I am always learning from the neurodivergent community to speak on their behalf, the views in this book are mine. If you are neurodivergent and your opinions are different, that is totally valid. You decide how you identify yourself, how you are treated and how your voice is used. Do not let anyone silence you. If you are neurotypical, however, it is time to take a step back and allow us to be heard.

This book is equal parts my story and your story. My hope is that you will see yourself in this journey and, as we celebrate the importance of embracing what's different about ourselves—our skills and abilities, the beauty of our minds—you will find your voice and your pathway to thriving in a world that so often doesn't make sense.

As a young girl sitting in a psychologist's office after receiving a diagnosis, I wish I had been handed this book. So, if that is you right now, hey, I see you. I was you. And I'm excited for the journey you're about to embark on.

This book is for any human who has thought for far too long that they're living on a planet that was not created for them and is wondering how they can find their way home. It's for those who are ready to take their place in their fairytale. It's for those who are ready to discover that they are *different*, but *not less.*

This book is also for the sidekicks in our stories, for every protagonist in a fairytale has their sidekicks. So, listen up parents, carers, wider family, friends, health professionals, teachers and the rest of you: you all have your parts to play. We can all be inspired to create a world in which *everyone* has the opportunity to succeed in all that we do.

So, find your favourite spot, get your favourite beverage (I quite fancy a matcha tea myself but, hey, it's your fairytale, so take your pick). The classical music is about to begin, the knight's horses have been tacked up in their finest leathers, the princess has been laced into her favourite dress.

You are about to embark on the greatest story: the one of you embracing who you are.

CHAPTER 1

Growing Up 'Quirky'

In the story of *The Lion King* (an absolute cult classic with arguably one of the best movie soundtracks of all time—thank you, Mr Elton John and Mr Hans Zimmer) we meet Simba, a sassy, confident, proud little lion cub with the most brilliant life any kid could possibly dream of. He spends his days training to become the king of Africa and playing in the grass with his friend Nala, and he's surrounded by a family that shows him nothing but love and protection. He grows up knowing that all of him, and all that he is, is good.

Simba's Once Upon a Time seems to be picture-perfect. Until it's not. At exactly thirty-five minutes and twenty-six seconds into the film, one of the saddest moments in cinematic history unfolds as Simba's uncle throws a whole 'long live the king' moment and this little lion cub's life changes forever. Simba's dad is killed, and he's blamed for it.

He's not off to a good start.

In *Aladdin*, we meet Genie, a bubbly, bold, louder-than-life character who seems to exist solely for comedic value. But behind the absolutely banger songs and quality one-liners, the Genie is going through something that makes even a street rat look like a prince. Genie is trapped, and he's been trapped for ten thousand years. He lives his life as a prisoner, accepting that this is all he will ever be.

He's not off to a good start.

In *The Hunchback of Notre Dame*, we meet Quasimodo. From the moment we see the title of this film, we know how Quasi has been created to be portrayed. People laugh at him and spit at him on the streets, and he's locked away in a bell tower because of what society tells him he is, and what he will never be. From day one, Quasimodo lives in a world that can never see him for who he is, and will only ever see him through myopic eyes as a monster. A burden. Different.

He's not off to a good start.

My Once Upon a Time was a bit difficult, too.

My parents called me 'our quirky little genius', 'our princess and the pea child'. This was because every night I was lost in my encyclopedias, later rambling about the facts I'd learned to anyone who cared (or didn't care) to listen. I would cry at the smallest sign of a tag touching my skin. And I couldn't make a single friend unless it was a snail I'd picked up on a path and begged to keep as a best friend.

I didn't fit in at school, my teachers often calling my parents to let them know that I'd spent all day hiding in the back of the library or in the toilet. I couldn't wear certain clothes, or deal with certain textures—my outfit of choice was Kmart tracksuits with the tags cut off. The only food that passed my lips was white, bland and less than two ingredients. (Pasta with cheese? Fine. White bread and butter? Great. Don't even *think* about adding something else into the mix, though.)

I didn't have any friends, nor did I care to try making them, and would instead be spellbound for hours in my books or make-believe worlds, which no one else was authorised to enter. I'd speak out of turn, lecturing adults as a seven year old and letting them know that their hair was messy, or that something they'd said was untrue, or that they were unkind. Other times, I'd go out of my way to tell every stranger I saw how pretty they were. And sometimes I wasn't able to speak at all, becoming mute.

Routine and structure were important; perish the thought of plans or routines changing. Something as small as dinner being ten minutes later than when Mum had said it would be, or the time of my weekly horse-riding lessons being moved would cause a panic equivalent to being caught in the headlights of an oncoming car.

I refused to walk down the laundry aisle in the grocery store because the smells made me want to vomit. Haircut appointments ended with me sobbing, taking multiple showers to rid myself of the feeling of hair snippets on my skin. And I begged to stay in the car whenever Mum went into a shop that I associated with the overpowering noise of overhead fluorescent lights.

Despite all of this, to my parents and those who surrounded me, I was just *Chloé*. A bit sensitive, a bit quirky, a bit off the cuff. And, after all, what child isn't a bit of an oddball?

To me, though? It felt like I had crash-landed on an alien planet, a world that seemed similar enough to my own that I was able to fake it for a few years, but distant enough that I felt like a complete and utter freak. It was as though everyone else had figured out the rules of this planet, but the rocket scientists back home had forgotten to give me the handbook, and it was entirely up to me to figure them out.

People on this planet were horribly, ridiculously confusing, and everything seemed like it was out to destroy my entire being. The lights were atrociously loud and blindingly bright. The people said things they didn't mean at all ('It's raining cats and dogs' apparently did not mean a hailstorm of puppies and kittens, much to my twelve-year-old self's disappointment). There were social 'rules' that everyone had to follow, even though they didn't make any sense and, if you broke them, people treated you as if you had just broken some secret, ancient code.

Eye contact? Small talk? And why are you people so touch oriented?

None of it made any sense. Even still, none of it makes sense.

For the longest time, I was convinced that my life was the furthest thing from a fairytale that it could possibly be. I was bewildered as to why my home planet had left me on this strange new planet where nothing added up and the things that should be were not, and the things that should not be, were. I was an alien trapped on a strange, confusing place far from home, alone and desperate, but every portal home had a big red 'No Chloés allowed' sign.

Still, to my parents, none of this seemed apparent, despite every part of my existence screaming 'autistic', like a bright, neon sign plastered to my forehead. I remained, simply, Chloé. *Weird, quirky, Chloé.*

Not off to a good start

I knew from a very young age that my mind was worlds apart from those of the people surrounding me. I knew it when I sat alone in the kindergarten playground and spoke to the birds while wistfully watching the other kids play. How did they make it look so easy? I knew it when the other kids built fantasy worlds out of LEGO while I lined the bricks up in colour order. I knew it when children my age walked past and I held Mum's hand a bit tighter, already (at the ripe old age of four) painfully aware of the judgemental stares and whispers. I knew that society didn't accept me, that I wasn't built for the culture our world had created.

I vividly remember writing a letter to God in my journal when I was five, asking why he'd made me so different, and if he could 'magic me' to not be so different, if it wasn't too much of a hassle. The idea of being different was terrifying, and the realisation that I might *always* be different led to tears, panic and a desperation for change. I became selectively mute for much of the first sixteen years of my life. What was the point of using my voice when I was convinced my existence wasn't needed?

Despite my early understanding that 'different' meant being ridiculed, it wasn't something anyone else worried about back then. Difference was seen as, 'You've yet to grow into yourself, but don't worry, it'll happen.' It wasn't entirely frowned upon for a child to be quirky. There is always a social quota on what level of 'odd', 'different', 'a bit of a screw loose' is deemed socially acceptable for kids. So, for some time, I was the only one who realised I was in an alien universe. The rest of the world would pat my parents on the back and assure them, 'Don't worry, she'll change'.

As is the way for so many of us who grow up different.

Of course, this isn't something limited to neurodivergence, it's something that so many of us face from the moment we're born. Different minds, bodies, identities . . . they're picked apart, as we either learn to conform or grow numb to the feeling of being alienated.

Little boys are taught that emotions are weak, that being 'manly' means being strong, tough and dominant.

Little girls are taught that being pretty is all they need to be, and that cooking, cleaning and mothering skills are more important than a brilliant mind, empowerment and independence.

Young BIPOC (black, indigenous and people of colour) children grow up with white Barbie dolls, cream-coloured stockings, white standards of beauty and a culture that implicitly privileges whiteness.

Heteronormativity is pushed on children from the moment they're born, and God forbid if a little girl wants to marry a princess instead of a prince—or no one at all.

Every single one of us is given a black and white manual of how and who we have to be in every aspect of our lives. Some of us are comfortable with that manual; our neurotypes, cultures and identities already fit with what our family, peers and culture see as 'normal'. These invisible rules are accepted and followed. But for those who can't, or don't, or choose not to, the script often starts like this:

> 'You're too young to understand.'
> 'You'll grow to accept it.'
> 'Oh well, life isn't fair.'

Society assumes that eventually we'll fade into an acceptance of what we *should* be, that we'll silence ourselves into a submission of the ideologies and expectations we've been taught. Divergent thoughts, ideas and emotions are pushed aside with the idea that eventually we'll learn to simply conform. We're taught that if a child thinks or acts out of the norm, don't worry, because they'll soon change their ways. Society often accepts difference in children, but it's not 'acceptance' so much as it is a confidence that those differences will fade.

But what about when they don't fade as the years pass? What happens when that child becomes a teenager, and societal pressure hasn't been enough to change their identity? That's when 'a little bit quirky' may as well be a form of the plague.

Challenging times

Being a teenager is difficult for even the most social, bubbly, 'totally got this' sort of person. You're in that weird limbo stage between childhood and adulthood, not allowed to do some things but expected to do others. It's expected that you'll start to discover yourself and your identity (but, not too much). You're finding out who you are, how to fit in, what your place in the world is and, perhaps, how different you are.

As a teenager, 'different' is synonymous with social reject, outcast, weirdo, loser . . . you get the point. It's social suicide. For me, it went from, 'Oh, that's Chloé. She's a bit quirky' to 'There's something wrong with that girl'. And the other teenagers Ate. That. Up.

Now, in my fairytale, instead of being like the little lion cub, I was the dead antelope carcass that lion cubs would eat . . . but they weren't lion cubs, they were hungry hyenas disguised as teenagers.

I spent Year 7 at a beachy high school where every single girl in my grade was curvy and skinny in all the right places, with bleached blonde hair and a perfect suntan, and all the boys were surfers, skaters or Harry Styles lookalikes. Everybody seemed to conform to an invisible manual of societal acceptance and didn't appear to question it (or, at the very least, did a wonderful job of playing pretend).

Conversely, I turned up to school with unbrushed hair and a piece of hay in it from feeding my horses that morning (the only thing that kept me sane). Instead of going to the local cafe or shopping centre after school with the rest of the girls, I'd catch the bus home and immediately retreat to my room to write make-believe stories, read my encyclopaedias or bribe my little sister into playing toy horses with me. So, yeah, popularity wasn't really beckoning me. Or even the idea of a basic social life, really.

It seemed that over the summer everyone had left me behind, the smoke of their Barbie car tyres blowing in my face, making very clear what I had already known for my entire life: I definitely, absolutely, 100 per cent was not created for this world. No matter how much I tried, no matter how much I pretended, no matter how much I fake-laughed and mimicked the personalities of the 'it girls', my childhood quirkiness was no longer accepted and it was time to conform. *Difference? Individuality? In this economy? Puh-lease.*

Society often accepts difference in children, but it's not 'acceptance' so much as it is a confidence that those differences will fade.

Finding our space

Our world teaches us that if we don't fit in, we'll be cast out. We're pushed into a tiny little box that we need to fit into to have a stable life. Some fit into that box quite easily; it was designed to fit them. Others manipulate and shift themselves to squeeze into it—and perhaps it's not exactly comfortable, but they can make it happen for the benefit of their lives, their futures, their careers, their relationships. But for some of us—many of us, actually—no matter how hard we contort, manipulate and squeeze, we simply cannot fit. It was not designed for our shape.

Children grow up terrified of being different, knowing that one day they're going to have to squeeze their beautifully creative, divergent minds and identities into a space that should never have been created in the first place. And it only makes sense for the adults in our lives to encourage this—it's the system they've always known, the same one they experienced. You want the best for your child, and it's accepted that the best is minimising yourself. *Do what you're told so you can survive.*

But why was this box created in the first place? And why can't we simply change the shape to fit each of us, as individuals?

Short answer: we can. We've simply accepted that it's easier and safer not to.

The idea of accepting difference is something we can do every day, and it starts with us. Teach the children in your life that their differences, their quirks, their 'out of the box' shapes are accepted, and learn to accept them within yourself, too—despite the fact that you've been taught to push them aside and hide them until they don't even feel a part of you anymore. Surround yourself with people who boldly embrace difference and what is uniquely them, both within your circle of people and in what you ingest via social and traditional media. Curate your Instagram feed and fill your bookshelves with humans of different body types, neurotypes, sexualities, genders, ethnicities . . . create a new normal.

It is time to create a society that understands that diversity in all aspects of life is something that we need, and that we cannot progress without difference.

It starts with us.

CHAPTER 2

School

It's common for kids to feel a little bit anxious on their first day of school—to hold on to their parent's hand tightly, cry for the first few minutes, protest that they'd rather stay home. The largeness of a school building, hundreds of other kids and the idea that things are changing from what they've known in their short little life is expected to come with a small amount of uncertainty.

It's also expected that the little worries would soon be quelled, that the tears would stop when they see the playground or the other kids, or their teacher and the craft supplies waiting for them. Then the hand will be let go of and the child will be off on their merry way with their lunchbox and a backpack three times the size of their bodies, ready to start thirteen years of education with a toothy little smile.

Yeah . . . that never happened for me.

The first week of hell . . . I mean, school

What was my school experience like? How was *my* first day of school?

Picture this: a gladiator showdown. I was both the ferocious lion and the puny little 'how did I end up in this situation' human. The school was the Colosseum, and my soon-to-be classmates the spectators who had unknowingly bought tickets to the most exhilarating, thrilling, untamed battle the world had ever seen.

Imagine me, beautifully brushed plaits on either side of my head. Much to my dismay, that had been my warm-up battle. My mother had begged, pleaded and finally bribed me into sitting still so she could brush my hair and plait it—to 'look lovely on my first day of big-kid school'. Schoolbag in tow, parent on either side, I looked like a prisoner on her way to death row.

In the process of merely getting me out of the car and to the school gates, I had grabbed on to any and all possible surfaces, kicking my legs and screaming bloody murder, hoping the nearby police station would hear my wails, assume kidnap or torture, and rescue me. The fiery pits of primary school hell were out to get me and I was not going to let them take me down without throwing every inch of my little four-year-old self into it along the way. This was war.

I. Was. Spartacus.

When I was dragged into the school building, I executed my final great feat with all the strength that a scrawny four year old could muster. I held on to the metal posts outside of the receptionist's office with such strength and determination that my parents started pulling one leg, and a school receptionist and principal pulled the other. It was like one of those children's cartoons, with my body parallel to the ground. Letting go was not an option.

The school staff, apparently accustomed to this sort of behaviour (although I like to think my battle was among the best they'd seen), barely batted an eyelid. After a few minutes, they decided that the fight wasn't worth having and reassured my parents that this was very normal, and that after they left I would drop the act, give in and go to class.

Tearfully, my parents left, as did the staff, who returned inside. I assume I was expected to admit defeat, let go of the bar, wipe my teary, mucus-covered face and walk inside with a solemn apology, ready for my first day of education. What really happened was similar to what Buddhist monks perhaps experience, or Spirit, the wild stallion of the Cimarron from the DreamWorks movie, in the scene when he was tied up to the fence without food and water for three days. Or maybe the protestors of great causes who stay put in the face of adversity. My stubborn, terrified little self did not budge.

I did not move a muscle that entire school day. My legs and arms were still wrapped around that metal bar when my parents returned six hours later.

That whole 'she'll get over it' idea? Nope, didn't happen.

I knew from day dot that school was going to be complete and utter hell, and I was right to cling on to that bar because the horrors that awaited were beyond what even my imagination could muster.

On the second day of school, I was convinced to let go of my beloved metal bar, thanks to an amber necklace my uncle had made for me and my cherished soft panda, which I'd had since I was an infant. Panda stayed with me the entire time, refusing to leave my arms even for a moment. Any suggestions from my teachers of 'letting her sleep in your bag until home time' were met with death stares filled with the same amount of poison as a golden dart frog (for those who don't have an animal hyper-fixation, that's a lot of poison).

My school was a devout Catholic school, a place where mass services and confessions of our sins happened every morning, where Jesus was a mysterious, untouchable entity reserved only for those holy enough to speak to him—or us commoners if we were given special selection. During morning prayers, the school priest would come to our classroom to light a candle that represented Jesus, then we would stand in a circle and the teacher would pass the candle (meaning Jesus) around so we could all pray. On my third day of school, I was handed the candle and, whether because of nerves, allergies or Satan himself infiltrating my spirit, I sneezed. I single-handedly blew out Jesus.

My teacher screamed and pointed me down like a fourteenth-century witch, yelling that, because of me, none of us would be able to pray that day, and that I was the sole reason why every single one of them was going to end up in hell. A bit of pressure to put on a four year old, hey? *Sorry for damning all of our spirits, guys. That one's on me.*

I was escorted to the priest's office and made to confess my sin of blowing out Jesus. I was then prayed for, so that Jesus would hopefully forgive me and save me from eternal damnation.

A small group of girls came up to me during lunch that day and asked if I wanted to play with them. I was still shaken by the whole candle blowing-out episode and I'd spent the day before sitting by myself, watching other kids interacting and creating friendships. I was desperate for the same thing, so I took their offer with an eager smile and Panda gripped in my arms.

After playing tag and hide and seek, one of the girls suggested we take turns hiding Panda to spice things up a little. How was I to know that a group of four- and five-year-old girls could be anything other than genuine? So, with a little kiss to Panda's forehead, I agreed and reluctantly handed her to one of the girls. Come the end of lunchtime, the too-loud school bell alerted us it was time to go in . . . and Panda was nowhere to be seen. Still cautiously optimistic, I asked the girls where she was. I was met with hurtful laughs, and then one of them told me that Panda had been thrown over the boundary and into the forest beside the school property.

Every part of me went numb. The forest next to the school was thick, untouched land with large banks and ditches, and impossible to get into. Still, I turned and ran back to the playground and tried to climb over the fence to get Panda back. The fence was several metres high and lined with barbed wire, but that wasn't going to stop me. I was fuelled with a determination that no barrier, no fence, no four-year-old bully could tear from me.

It didn't take long for the teachers to realise I wasn't in class and to find me bawling my eyes out, desperately trying to get over the fence. 'Oh well, that's what happens when you bring precious items to school,' they answered to my tearful plight, dragging me back to class. Even now, writing about this makes my heart sink and my eyes feel sharp with tears.

After school that day, Mum and I found Panda hidden underneath a pile of tanbark in the playground cubby house.

On my fourth day, during lunch, I was invited to play basketball with another group of kids. I naively agreed and was then beaten up by some boys while the girls stood by, watched and chanted. I went home without speaking of the incident. There hadn't been any adult witnesses, and I'd already learned how little the teachers cared for me and how much of a mess-up they thought I was. When my parents asked how school was that day, I responded with a quiet 'fine' and retreated to my room.

On my fifth day, again during lunch, my amber necklace was violently ripped from my neck, little orange beads flying everywhere. As the school bell screeched, I attempted to collect the beads that had been thrown in varying directions, now blending in with the tanbark and becoming twice as difficult to spot with the tears pooling in my eyes. I was once again dragged back to class—this time given detention for disobeying school rules.

And that was just my first week.

Honestly, looking back, I probably deserved all this after a horrible, awful, unforgivable thing I did in blowing out Jesus. *Sorry, again.*

So, yeah. It took me all of one week to realise that school completely, utterly sucked. I should have kept holding on to that metal post after all.

The never-ending school adventure

School didn't get any easier. If anything, I learned over and over how broken the system is and how overlooked we are if we can't conform—not just by the educational system, but by teachers and students who have been taught that fitting in is the only way to amount to anything and who will ridicule, condemn and destroy anyone who doesn't.

It didn't take long for me to become paranoid and fearful of school. I stopped speaking up in class, scared to put my hand up if I didn't understand a question for fear of the teacher calling me lazy, stupid or inattentive (all of which happened multiple times). You don't know true suffering until you've been belted over the head with *The Complete Works Of Shakespeare* by an angry teacher who's trying to beat the 'quirky' out of you, or whipped on the knuckles for not touch-typing fast enough (although I can now type over 135 words a minute, so thanks, I suppose), or have slurs yelled at you by a substitute teacher for being 'either deaf, retarded or really, really dumb. Take your pick.' *Absolutely correct. I should not have been born different, that's on me. Sorry, once again.*

Not speaking in class soon turned into not showing up for class, spending many days hiding in the toilets or at the back of the library. When my hiding spots were discovered, not going to class turned into not going to school. I got away with it for a while, able to fake a stellar cough and sick voice. But as time progressed and my parents grew suspicious, I took it up a notch.

As a child, and even now still, I can get myself so worked up, so worried and paranoid, that I become physically sick. Growing up, my parents could always tell when I was lying because, within seconds of the lie coming out, I would be absolutely chucking my guts. Now as an adult, I know when I'm overworking myself or becoming stressed because I'll get chronic tonsillitis, something I had at least five times a year as a child, too. When it came to school, the very idea of going to a place that was so horrendously toxic caused my body to turn on itself, and so, when I complained to Mum and Dad of feeling ill and getting migraines, it wasn't a lie.

Avoiding school dominated such a large part of my time I hardly ever went. Over time, I could stop even pretending to be sick in order to stay home and was simply allowed to. I think Mum started to realise how uncomfortable school was for me, and the effect it was having on my mental health. So, if allowing her daughter to stay in her room and learn by writing exuberant stories and reading adult-length novels and university-grade encyclopaedias was what it took, so be it.

As lovely as that was, it's illegal for a child to miss more than a certain number of schooldays per year, a number that I had well and truly overshot by the end of term one. There was no permanent escape for me. When I was there teachers would praise and reward the children with perfect attendance while looking at me with disdain.

The concept of attendance policies—pizza parties, ribbons and awards for children who turn up every day—has never sat right with me. It doesn't give disabled, chronically ill or mentally ill children fair opportunity. In fact, it penalises them for being less healthy or capable, compromising the safety of immunocompromised children and those whose minds and bodies can't deal with the stress of the system. It's a concept rooted deeply in ableism (discrimination that favours neurotypical and able-bodied people) and doesn't place any value on actual education, which, as I came to discover, is true for many things in the schooling system. Go figure.

One day in Year 3, I was sitting on my bedroom floor at home playing an elaborate game with my toy horses when I heard a knock at the door. There, standing in my doorway, were the school principal and two other staff members. My heart dropped. I immediately felt bile rise to my throat, my body begin to shake and the back of my eyes stinging with tears as the teachers put on sweet voices, feigning interest in my horses before breaking the news that I needed to go to school. That 'no' wouldn't be accepted as an answer, and they were here to take me there now. I cried my eyes out, begging them to let me stay home and pleading with Mum, who had tears in her own eyes, to make them go away as they dragged me to their car to take me to school—not even that metal bar could save me now.

My one and only saving grace at school came in Year 4 in the form of one teacher: *Wendy.* Despite never knowing a diagnosis for my difference, she never cared, nor did she ever try to make me conform. Instead, Wendy praised my differences daily and made sure that, during her class, I was never left feeling like an outcast.

Wendy quickly noticed that I learned differently from the other students, and always made time to explain things in a way I understood. We used little signals so I wouldn't feel exposed when I felt overwhelmed or uncertain. She allowed me to sit wherever I needed, to learn in the ways I needed, and she made exceptions in our school projects, so I was allowed to write about the subjects that made me tick.

During lunch, Wendy would give up her own personal time to let me sit in the classroom with her, where the two of us would discuss our favourite books and animals, and she'd listen to my rambles about horses and the *Titanic*. On particularly bad days, she'd hug me, dry my tears, reassure me, and tell me to pull out a book to clear my head. On multiple occasions, she even brought her rescued Border Collie into school and allowed her to sit beside me throughout the day so I would feel less vulnerable and scared.

When I couldn't attend school for days at a time due to anxiety and fear, she'd greet me back with open arms, asking, 'How are you feeling? How can I help? I missed you.' She actively encouraged me to pursue whatever made my heart sing, reminding me on multiple occasions that school was only one chapter of my life, and in the real world I would find my people and my place, and thrive.

Throughout my nine years of mainstream schooling, Wendy was the only teacher who encouraged me to be *me*, who showed me that who I was wasn't only okay but was also wonderful. I still think of Wendy all the time and will never forget the impact she had on me. She was that one teacher who instrumentally shifted my life, who taught me that it wasn't the whole world that was bad. We just need to look for our sidekicks. Wendy was my first sidekick, and the only one I ever had within the schooling system.

A system of sameness

And then came Year 7—high school. High school was a completely new ballgame, a battle that would make my primary school struggles seem like child's play. Petty bullying, stealing Panda and mocking my name ('Chlo-wee' was a classic gag, apparently) turned into harmful insults. Suddenly, it wasn't just 'Chloé's weird', it was:

'Chloé's fat.'
'Chloé's ugly.'
'Chloé's dumb.'
'Why are your eyes so wide apart?'
'Why does your nose look like that?'
'You're never going to get a boyfriend.'
'You shouldn't even be here.'

It was letters put in my locker telling me to kill myself. It was that same locker being broken into, my books stolen, and my art books drawn all over, then teachers telling me I should have had a better locker combination and to not allow myself to be such an easy target.

It was a boy looking pointedly at me during debate class while stating that 'abortions should have been made legal', and girls writing fake notes impersonating me and then putting them into popular boys' lockers, making me the laughing stock.

It was teachers pulling me aside and telling me, 'You're in high school, you need to grow up', and giving me detention when I got teary for not understanding the lessons.

It was having my clothes stolen during Phys Ed, a necklace I had been gifted for my thirteenth birthday being ripped off and thrown into the ocean, and a baby bird that I had rescued and hidden in my blazer pocket crushed in front of my eyes when someone yelled out to the teacher that 'Chloé was playing on her phone under the desk' when I was actually feeding him mashed worms.

It was being pushed into the shallow end of the pool during school sports day, my two front teeth cracked and falling out while the boys laughed. It was teachers yelling at me for being a smart-arse because I answered a math question that asked, 'How long it would take for a frog to get to a pond a kilometre away if it jumped a certain distance each day?' by writing a full page explaining that the frog would die before it got to the pond because amphibians can't go more than three days without water.

It was consistent reports of 'She's incredibly intelligent, but disordered and doesn't fit in with her peers at all. She needs to try harder', of teachers banning me from certain classes, and of me becoming violently sick most days because of the fear, sadness and anxiety that came with school.

I ended up attending more than ten different schools in eight years, my parents convinced each and every time that they simply hadn't found the right one. We tried schools that had more than a thousand students per year level and others with only fifty on the entire campus. We tried fancy private schools with equestrian teams, and public schools where 'after-school activities' meant snorting a line behind the school building. We tried city schools and schools on thousand-acre farms where our daily school chores included wrangling lambs . . . and still, nothing ever changed.

What I learned was that it does not matter what you do, or where you go, schools are all organised around the same basic system. It's a system that will never work for a neurodivergent person, no matter how hard they try, because its entire foundation is built against us—despite the fact that, on average, up to 30 per cent of students in a class are neurodivergent.

School is created on a system that supports, encourages and praises sameness. Children are taught that they have to perform, act, behave and be a certain way or they'll never be able to survive in the world. I can't count the number of times a teacher laughed at my struggles and said, 'If you think this is difficult, wait until you're in the real world'.

But the thing is, the real world is nothing like school.

In the adult world, no two of us learn the same, have the same job, think the same, perform the same or are expected to have the same lives, careers and working styles. That's why some people thrive in office jobs while others thrive as farmers, marine biologists, directors, engineers or chefs. We can't expect a farmer to work an office job, or a computer tech to be an actor, so why do we expect children, during the most vulnerable point of their developmental lives, to meet this criterion?

Why do we pressure children to fit inside one single box when society isn't built for us to be like that?

Children are failed by the school system every day. Autistic kids, ADHD kids and children with all forms of neurodiversity who are vastly intelligent and so ready to learn but are never given the opportunity to do so because our system refuses to support them. I'm not sure why.

Maybe it's too inconvenient for teachers to give those extra few minutes to check in, to make sure we're okay, to make sure the lesson plans actually make sense. Or maybe it's because the school system is designed to program us into sameness, rather than allow us to use our unique creativity, intelligence and perspectives. Most likely it's a mixture, and also because we, as a society, have preconceived ideas of what we have to be like, and if we're not that, we're useless.

Whatever the reason, it's not good enough. We will never get anywhere with a system that refuses to embrace difference.

After nine years of struggling in a system that had failed me, my body and mind slowly dying, my autism diagnosis in Year 8 could not have come soon enough. Still, I wasn't removed from the school system until my parents sat down with the psychologist who diagnosed me and heard these words: 'You need to remove your daughter from school now, or you won't have a daughter anymore.'

For the first time since starting school, I felt free. I went to bed that night without the ache in my stomach and the throbbing in my head reminding me of the school bus coming the following morning. I never again had to lay out my itchy uniform at the end of my bed, or feel my head grow dizzy as I stepped through those school gates.

Mum and Dad have told me that from the very first day I was homeschooled, a sparkle came back into my eyes.

Why do we pressure children to fit inside one single box when society isn't built for us to be like that?

How homeschooling saved me

A lot of people have very odd ideas about homeschooling, or alternative education as a whole.

It's not real education

False. Alternative schooling that allows children to learn, grow and develop at their own pace and in their own environment can do nothing but good. I learned exactly what I needed to learn to bring me further along in life—more so than a mainstream school could ever teach me . . . and I did it in a way that wasn't detrimental to my own health. *That* is real education.

The child will become a socially outcast freak

I spent so much of my school life locked inside a bathroom, being mentally tormented or physically hurt by other students and teachers. Becoming a socially outcast freak was the least of my worries.

How will they ever make friends?

Kids at school often have nothing in common other than the fact that they live in the same district and are the same age. How is that enough to deem someone friendship-worthy? While getting homeschooled, I made friends at my own pace, in my own environments. Over time, my fear of people began to ease and I found myself choosing to step out into the world.

I made friends at a pony club, where I could speak to people about ponies for hours. I made friends at a camera club, where I sat down and eagerly spoke about camera settings and favourite photography spots with 85-year-old retirees over a cuppa. I made friends at Riding for the Disabled, where I became the state's youngest volunteer and teacher. I made friends at acting and singing class, where my quirks and oddities were praised and encouraged, and where everyone else was equally bizarre.

All of these activities, by the way, granted me far more education than anything I'd been taught inside a classroom.

Throughout the last four and a half years of my schooling life, I excelled. While some subjects remained troublesome—meltdowns over long division were inevitable, and some days proved to be too difficult—nothing ever flared to the point that it had while I was inside a classroom.

On the 'my brain's not working today' days, I'd learn out in the world, going on road trips with Dad, or spending the day in my pony's paddock with an encyclopaedia in hand, identifying and drawing bugs and flowers and birds.

On the 'I just don't get it' days, Mum and Dad would sit with me for hours to make sure things were explained in ways that I understood. When a math question asked me to 'List two different ways to give the customer $17.50 worth of change' and I became a crying mess, protesting, 'But this isn't a math question! You either throw it in their face or hand it to them politely', my parents simply laughed with me and explained what it *actually* meant—rather than yell and put me in detention.

I was allowed to be wholeheartedly, unashamedly myself and, because of this, I thrived. I graduated high school with academic awards in English, art and (proof that Jesus doesn't hate me for blowing him out) math. A year later, I even decided to go back to a mainstream college to study Christianity, philosophy, leadership and creative arts—but this time, I knew who I was and how to stand up for myself when the system didn't stand up for me. I knew that my mind, my learning style and my entire being were okay, accepted and important.

I was incredibly privileged to have parents in a position to homeschool me, and to have a support network that understood and accepted my differences rather than continue to force me into an institution that would never work for me. However, it's not fair that the only options we currently have for children like me is to either have their parents give over their lives to homeschooling, or to suffer in an environment where every ounce of them is ridiculed, ripped apart or forced to change.

Changing the system

I've come out the other side of the schooling system now, and I'm okay—I survived. But I'm still hearing about and seeing first-hand the abuse and neglect that happen to young neurodivergent folk in schools every single day. Young kids are experiencing chronic mental illness; eight year olds are suicidal because they're spending five days a week in facilities where they're mistreated, tormented and abused. Teenagers leave school feeling worthless and like they are burdens on society because they've never been taught correctly. And because that is exactly what the school system has taught us to believe. We are being hurt by the same system that was created to help us.

Educationally, autistic children have the worst outcomes of all disabled students in the schooling system, with 97 per cent facing difficulties in their education and 56 per cent saying they're being treated unfairly. Forty-four per cent of autistic children change schools multiple times to try and find a place that caters to them, and 35 per cent will not continue their education past Year 10. These statistics are not just 'part of being autistic' or 'part of being disabled'. These statistics are *only* because our system refuses to support children who are different.

Our curriculum *needs* to change.

We need to change assessment techniques. Teachers need to be educated about disabilities and neurodiversity as part of their training. We need to demand extra support in and out of the classroom; there is no excuse for inaccessibility. Neurodivergent children deserve an educational system in which we feel safe, validated and have the ability to thrive just as much as our neurotypical peers.

I still sometimes struggle to pick up my siblings from school or go to their school recitals because the fear school buildings imprinted upon me has impacted my mental health and relationship with the education system for the rest of my life.

I still feel my heart jump an extra hundred beats and tears prick my eyes when I'm asked to speak to groups of teachers about what the school system needs to do to improve.

I still have to fight judgement and prejudice because of what our education system has instilled into all of us about people who are different like me—that because I'm not built like others, my mind is wrong.

If you judge a fish's ability to climb a tree, it will live its whole life thinking it's stupid. And if you put a brilliant, neurodiverse child into an institution where they are forced to conform, they will live their whole life thinking they're worthless.

CHAPTER 3

Sensory Issues, Stimming, Meltdowns, Shutdowns and Burnout

SENSORY ISSUES, STIMMING, MELTDOWNS, SHUTDOWNS AND BURNOUT

Stimming, sensory issues, meltdowns, burnout ... Ah, the sweet words that come with a brain that wasn't created to fit into a neurotypical world. But what do they all mean? What can we do to best support ourselves and the neurodivergent folk in our lives when it comes to our minds and our bodies' reactions to the world around us? And, what happens when we don't receive that support?

In a world that is geared towards its neurotypical members, and diminishes, deflects and degrades its neurodivergent ones, how can we possibly survive? How can we get by?

This chapter discusses the not so great, 'ah heck' moments of a neurodivergent brain in a neurotypical world.

Strap in, folks. This one's a wild, wild ride.

Sensory issues

Our senses are what we use to experience, interact with and perceive the world around us. We use our eyes, ears, tongue, nose and skin in different ways, but the overall purpose of these organs is to utilise our senses to recognise, navigate and work in our surrounding environments. This information, and the way our minds translate it, is called 'sensory processing'.

The way we take in sensory input is different for everyone, and no two people will process or use the information in the same way. While one person may love the feeling of sand between their toes, another may want to gag at the mere thought of it. While one person may love loud festivals and concerts, for another they may be a living nightmare.

Some of us use our ears to take in information around us; others use our senses of touch, or sight. For one person certain textures, smells or sounds may be unbearable, for another they may be barely noticeable.

Every day, we are constantly flooded with sensory stimuli: traffic noise, people talking, over a trillion detectable scents, an explosive rainbow of colour. A lot of people are able to filter out or 'folder' that stimuli in a way that is manageable. For some, however, simply surviving that input can feel like a mission to Mars (in a very loud rocket ship, with seats made of nails, and every possible smell bombarding us). This intense ability (or lack thereof) to process sensory input can impact the way we experience the world.

Imagine that you're at the loudest rock concert you've ever been to, right by the speakers, and the concert has been going on for three months without a break. Right in the middle of it you're expected to write an essay in a language you've never heard of. Alternatively, imagine that you're in an invisible isolation room with glass walls. You can see the world and the world can see you, but they can't see the glass walls. They're completely unaware of the chamber you're in. No matter what they say, you can't hear them, you can't feel them, you can't communicate. You're trapped, you're stuck, and you can't get out.

This *too much* or *too little* processing of stimuli is called sensory processing disorder, and it affects between 5 and 16 per cent of children, and up to 95 per cent of autistic people. With this disorder, our brains struggle to both receive and respond to the information that comes in through our senses. In groovy terms, our brain activity has an absolute party when we're exposed to different sensory stimuli. *Nice.*

Sensory issues have always plagued my life. The entire world is huge, and loud, and bright, and painful, and constant. Growing up, my mum wanted to dress me in expensive, frilly dresses and bows, but the feeling of the tag on my skin and the pressure on my head were enough to send me into fits. I felt like my skin was being pricked with nails, that my brain was about to explode out of my ears. I would rip the clothing off and refuse to get dressed unless it was in a matching fleece tracksuit set from Kmart—tags cut off.

When we went to the supermarket, I'd have to wait at the end of the laundry detergent aisle because the smells were so overpowering that it felt like my blood was Dynamo Superior Stain Remover and my lungs were Surf 5 in 1.

I was once at the hairdresser when the prickly feeling of little bits of hair in my clothes became so intense, all sense of rationality and correct social behaviour left me and I fully stripped in the middle of the shop, desperate to rid myself of the prickling fire on my skin.

Every time we attended a loud event, my brain would fizzle to the point of me passing out and having a seizure on the floor, ending up in a hospital emergency department on multiple occasions. I'd spend the following days in tears, vomiting and unable to stand. (On one occasion, this happened at church. The congregation thought I was overcome with the power of Christ and came to pray with me. I didn't have the heart to let them know that I was, in fact, just overcome by the power of the lights and music.)

On the other side of the coin, sometimes when my system is overwhelmed and overworked, my senses fade to the point of becoming utterly useless, particularly hearing and touch. When this affects me, my brain struggles to convert sensory input into translatable information, taking an extended amount of time to process the information being received. Often, I can't hear a single thing anyone is saying, making 'What did you say?' and 'Sorry, can you repeat that?' staples of my speech pattern. People tend to assume I'm purposely avoiding conversation, slow minded or choosing to not pay attention, particularly at school (*'incredibly poor listener and inattentive'* were staples on my report cards). I've taught myself to be a half-decent lip reader because life doesn't come with subtitles.

At times, the intensity of the world will affect all of my senses so deeply that my ability to speak disappears entirely.

This disorder, along with a fun little often-comorbid condition called 'dyspraxia', plays a part in my mind–body–senses mismatch. Dyspraxia is also caused by our brain signals not connecting to our bodies, and it affects gross motor skills, motor planning and coordination. It's generally a separately diagnosed condition, but a significant amount of neurodivergent folk, like me, have it. Consequently, my handwriting is absolutely shocking, food ends up on my clothes more frequently than it does in my mouth and I'm constantly covered in bruises from walking into doors, bumping into objects and not seeing what's right in front of me. I've fallen over my own feet and invisible objects more times than I can count, and my ability to drive is slim-to-none—my brain is unable to visualise the distance between myself and an object (not brilliant when you're driving head-on into traffic). If I had a dollar for every time I crashed a car in my first year of trying to drive, I'd have $8—not a lot of money, but a lot of car accidents.

If I'm given too many puzzle pieces of sensory stimuli to work out, my senses will often be disrupted and go home, abandoning me to fend for myself. I'm left to deal with awkward repercussions when my hearing stops working, or my hands and brain decide to have a heated, traumatic divorce, or I have the occasional fun little breakdown because my clothes are touching my body, or a piece of food didn't feel right in my mouth, or someone spoke in a frequency that made my brain hurt.

The overload that comes with sensory processing disorder is something that can be terrifying and debilitating, and it will usually stay with us throughout our entire lives. Sensory processing disorder, dyspraxia and all the other things surrounding our brain's inability to work in sync with our senses and bodies can impact our ability to perform to a socially accepted standard, whether at school, work or in our social lives.

While sensory processing disorder can be helped and altered by a change of environment and better understanding from the society around us, it's been made fairly clear that this sort of instrumental change isn't going to happen any time soon. So, in the meantime, there are ways that we can learn to live with it and combat it by learning more about ourselves, and learning more about teaching ourselves to validate, value and love our minds.

SIGNS OF SENSORY OVERLOAD

Loss of balance and poor coordination

As an overload of input is entering into our heads, it becomes increasingly difficult to remove it, which affects our balance and coordination.

Our brains give a little dramatic performance: *You know what? You're on your own. I'm going to a party but you're not invited.*

Our body responds with: *Motor skills? Coordination? What's that? Never heard of them.*

Changes in skin tone

With our bodies not taking in signals properly and growing stressed, we may start to show the physical signs of that discomfort: paleness, pink cheeks, sweating or shivers.

Becoming non-verbal

When we're in sensory overload and getting so many different inputs from so many different avenues, verbal communication can be the first thing to leave us. Translating our thoughts into verbal communication that you can hear and understand adds a new layer of difficulty, and with our brains somewhat hibernating to protect us, it can become close to impossible to speak.

In this situation, I have a set of communication cards for when I really need to communicate.

Racing heartbeat

A racing heartbeat can be a telltale sign of sensory overload, an anxiety attack or a panic attack. It's important to take time out, rest and practise mindful breathing when this happens. Ignoring it can lead to fainting, fits and the potential of a hospital visit, which is the absolute last thing you need if you're already in sensory overload.

That said, if a racing heart is something you experience frequently, please have a chat with your GP. Don't go through life with a potential undiagnosed medical condition just because a book told you it could be related to sensory overload.

Hysteria and crying

If you're getting to the point of hysteria, you probably don't need to be told that sensory overload may be imminent—by this point you're already well aware that it is. Ultimately, growing a deep understanding of your body will allow you to pick up on the signs of being overwhelmed before it gets to the point of hysteria. That said, these moments can sneak up on any of us. Get out of the situation and find a safe spot. Look after your mental health before anything else.

Cramps and nausea

When your brain starts to panic, your body starts to panic, which is why cramps, stomach pain, racing heart and changes in skin tone can all be signs of sensory overload. Again, if stomach pain is something you experience regularly, have a quick chat with your GP.

Repetition of words

Repetition of words (or 'echolalia') is incredibly common in autistic people, and during sensory overload this can be heightened. With so much input happening and without a brilliant ability to output it, echolalia can be both a soothing mechanism and a way to lock information in our heads.

Excessive stimming

Repetitive self-stimulatory behaviour (or 'stimming') helps us cope with sensory input, so it's only natural for that response to heighten when we're in uncomfortable situations. With so much happening around us, it can become physically painful, so we use stimming as a way to ground ourselves, self-soothe and try to make sense of everything that's happening.

It's important to note that stimming is a normal, positive part of the human experience, and should not be hidden if it's something that is going to benefit you. (For more on stimming, see page 47.)

Becoming agitated or angry

It only makes sense that, if you're having so much input coming at you and you're unable to process it, you'll get agitated. You'll get tired, drained, zoned out, and you'll want to get away from everything. When it's impossible to do that, becoming agitated, upset or angry is only natural.

Difficulty focusing

If sensory overload is happening in a classroom or workplace, it may become impossible to focus on work. If it's happening in a social setting, it may become impossible to focus on conversations and you may begin to drift away, zone out or repeat words and sentences.

HOW TO COPE WITH SENSORY OVERLOAD

Know the signs

Just as every human being is different, every person's sensory issues will be different, and every person's coping mechanisms will be different. It's important that you begin to form a relationship with your mind, and a deeper understanding of yourself and what sensory overload may look like for you. Do you start stimming more? Do you lose focus and zone out? Does your heart rate go up? Do loud noises suddenly become excruciating?

Over time, you'll learn what your first signs of overload are, which means you'll be better equipped to either deal with or leave the situation before things progress.

Set a game plan

If I know that I'm going to be in an environment that's extremely stimulating (such as a concert, party or festival), I'll make sure I have a game plan before I go. Most places will have a map, or at the very least someone you can ask, that will help you figure out your exit points and 'get outta here' areas before attending. So, if you need to leave, you'll have your escape route mapped out.

If you're running errands, have a list, stick to the list and plan your day and locations prior to going so you can easily escape if you need to. Don't further overload yourself with side trips or 'while I'm here' stops. Keep it simple and know how to get out.

I always have earplugs and noise-cancelling earbuds or headphones on hand. If the situation allows, I also carry stim toys and weighted lap blankets—whatever my body may need to get through the day without overloading my senses.

Adjust your environment

When you're in sensory overload, your body is telling you that all of your senses have had too much and can't handle anything that may up the intensity. You owe it to yourself to ensure that the environment you are in is helping these senses, rather than creating further hindrance. This means:

★ using low, soft, warm lighting—instead of overhead lights, use a salt lamp, a warm-toned desk lamp in the corner of the room, a night light or fairy lights
★ wearing comfortable clothing that isn't going to aggravate your mind or your body—for some people, tight compression clothing may be exactly what they need to help them feel grounded and in control. For others, it may be the loosest, baggiest clothing they can find.
★ having noise-cancelling headphones and gentle music, or decibel-reducing earplugs
★ scheduling your day to perfection, including breaks, eating and going to the toilet.

Listen to yourself, listen to your mind, listen to your body. What do you need? What do you need to stay away from? You're the expert on yourself, and it's important to surround yourself with things that will benefit you.

Stimming

Stimming, or self-stimulatory behaviour, seems to go hand in hand with an autism diagnosis and refers to repetitive movements or sounds. It's also something that seems to distress much of the neurotypical community. People hear the word 'stim', or see an autistic child self-regulating their body, and act as if their entire understanding of the human race has been altered and beaten to the ground. Common reactions are distaste, disgust and discomfort.

'Stop moving like that.'
'Act normal.'
'That's no way to behave in public.'

I've worked with doctors, psychologists and self-identified 'autism experts' who claim that stimming is a sign of poor behaviour and something we need to eradicate. Once, while taking part in a panel discussion, I was told by another panelist that my experience and knowledge were wrong and shouldn't be listened to because I was stimming as I spoke and was therefore 'uncured'. *Pardon me, I wasn't aware that flapping my hands had anything to do with my intelligence.*

Another time, when I was fiddling with my necklace at an event, I was slapped on the wrist by an older woman and told 'that's a horrid habit'. I was twenty-three years old and had *never* met the woman before.

People will see an autistic child rocking, flapping or making repetitive noises and immediately deem it as odd, weird, unnecessary and uncomfortable. Society has come to fear human beings simply moving their bodies in a way that doesn't suit its current understanding of 'normal'.

But, why? When we see someone acting in a way that's different from us, why do we automatically judge it as *wrong*? Particularly because stimming is an entirely normal part of the human experience.

The fact of the matter is: Every. Single. Person (in the entire history of the universe, *ever*). Stims.

Mic drop. *Take that, panel-man and weird-old-lady. You're just like me.*

Playing with your hair is stimming.
Clicking your pen is stimming.
Jiggling your leg is stimming.

The fact of the matter is:
Every. Single. Person
(in the entire history
of the universe, *ever*).
Stims.

Playing with the cord of your hoodie is stimming.

Twisting your ring is stimming.

Humming is stimming.

Tapping your pencil is stimming.

Chewing your lip is stimming.

Right now, as you read this very page, you are likely stimming. Because. It's. Natural.

We stim because we're focused, we're bored, we're stressed, we have pent-up emotions that need a place to escape. We do it because we're human beings who naturally need to move our bodies and ground ourselves.

The difference when it comes to autistic people, as with many things, is the *way* we stim. (As we've discussed, some people don't like things that are different, whether or not it affects them at all.) For autistic people, stimming may look like flapping our hands, rocking, jumping up and down, repeating sounds or words, twirling, walking on our toes, rubbing certain fabrics or rearranging objects.

Because of these different types of stims, there seems to be a mindset that stimming = bad. That it's something we need to stop, hide or eradicate.

To the teachers, psychologists, parents, panel-man, weird-old-lady and anyone reading this who is hoping that I'm about to present a foolproof method of erasing stims, forcing silence and conformity, you, my internalised-ableist friend, are about to be highly disappointed.

Stimming is *not* a bad thing. And not only should we not try to get rid of it, we should encourage it. If we continue to feed a society that doesn't value individuality and human beings as they are, we begin to destroy them.

While growing up, stimming was a part of my every day. I would flap my hands when I got excited, rock when I was upset, walk on my toes when I felt anxious and repeat sounds when I was overwhelmed. No one ever mentioned it, no one would ever bring it up or seemed to care about it, because it was just Chloé. That was just how I was. My parents often said I looked like a little fairy walking on my toes and flapping and jumping. When I was a toddler, Mum was convinced I must have been a dolphin in my past life because my echolalia seemed so like dolphin squeaks.

When a child does something regarded to be ever-so-slightly peculiar, it's not worried about too much. Children are allowed to be a little bit different, a little bit quirky, a little bit flappy.

> 'They'll grow out of it.'
> 'They'll learn.'
> 'Society will soon fix them.'

But as they get older and still don't learn to conform or hide, what was *different* becomes completely, absolutely unacceptable.

As I got older, it became apparent that moving my body in these ways was suddenly seen as an atrocity. I was viewed as a leper, someone unapproachable, someone who was barely functioning. I was Quasimodo, a monster. I was Genie, stared at in odd curiosity. I was Simba, cast out for something I couldn't change. If I began to stim, it was quickly silenced with a firm restraint of my hand or a quiet murmur: 'Stop it. People are going to think you're a lunatic.'

Oh. That was it.

This is why people (particularly parents) are so fearful of their children stimming. Our world has taught us that if we act in a way that is different to the social norm, we are considered low functioning, stupid, dumb, childish, *loony.* And the thing is, perhaps those fears are valid. No one wants to see their child ridiculed. But why are we then determined to change the child, rather than the world around them? Why do we validate the wrong just because it's normalised, and ostracise the right just because it's not?

So many people during my teenage years told me that I needed to stop stimming and start acting normal, would whisper and give side-eye glances in my direction. I was taught to conform, to mask, to cover up. I had to *behave* if I wanted any chance of survival.

And so, I did exactly that.

I hid and forced away any need to stim. *Neurodivergent? Not me. Wrong girl.*

My need to self-regulate was left unattended and silenced. I firmly pushed away what my mind and body desperately needed to do for fear of being further bullied and ridiculed. However, instead of these needs disappearing and me magically becoming 'normal', as was so desired by those around me, they turned into pent-up anxiety, depression and dysregulation that would end up bubbling over to the point of meltdowns.

My body would become so overwhelmed and panicked that meltdowns became a daily part of my life, I spent more time in tears than I did smiling. Pent-up stims changed into self-destructive behaviours that I couldn't control. Instead of flapping my hands, bouncing or repeating words, I would dig my fingernails into my skin until I bled, scratch myself until my skin was raw, hit the floor and bite my lips until they bled. I developed tics that made me jerk my neck to the point of long-term damage.

Taking away a child's stims doesn't take away their need to self-regulate; instead, it forces them into new habits that can cause long-term side effects and harm, including severe anxiety disorder, depression and emotional dysregulation. In 50 per cent of cases where therapy is used to stop an autistic child from stimming, the child has come out with symptoms that meet the criteria for post-traumatic stress disorder.

Fun fact: you can be a successful, functioning member of society while flapping your hands. If we try to stop neurodivergent people from stimming in ways that are non-harmful (such as rocking, flapping and jumping), the behaviour is not going to stop altogether; it will instead transfer to stims that *do* have the potential to become self-harmful.

Stimming is a normal, necessary part of human existence, and it's something we need to normalise, understand, accept and grow comfortable with. As I've gotten older and realised that society's expectations are only as firm as we allow them to be, I've discovered that allowing myself to unmask and be my authentic autistic self—stims and all—has unleashed more ability than I ever had when I was locking myself away.

Having the privilege to unmask and be myself was the hardest, the longest and one of the most important parts of my journey. I described this as 'privilege' because I'm aware that this is something many are not safely able to do yet. I'm able to unmask safely because of my support system, and the way I appear to the outside world. I have a support network that I know wholeheartedly loves the unfiltered, all-autistic version of me.

And, as a young, small, able-passing white woman, society doesn't see my authentic autistic self and the stims that come with that as a threat. If I stim, the worst that happens is the potential odd look in my direction, or a couple of nasty comments—things that aren't detrimental to my health or wellbeing in the big picture, mostly because I've learned that they are no reflection on me. However, if I didn't have that support system, my situation may not be the same. And if I were a larger male, specifically a larger male of colour, my body's natural need to cope in a world not created for me could be seen as threatening and dangerous, simply because of the stigma society has created around autism, disabilities and the people around us.

NEED TO STIM?

Visual stims

- ★ salt lamps, fairy lights, night lights, LED lights
- ★ kaleidoscopes, glitter lamps, lava lamps
- ★ calming videos (virtual fish tanks, sensory videos, visual ASMR)

Auditory stims

- ★ clicking or popping fidget toys
- ★ listening to music
- ★ ambient noise
- ★ echolalia
- ★ singing, reciting poetry/scripts/books

Tactile stims

- ★ fidget cubes, bubble wrap, spinner rings
- ★ soft toys, soft fabric
- ★ water beads, kinetic sand
- ★ room cleaning/rearranging

Chew stims

- ★ chewing gum
- ★ 'chewellery'

Vestibular stims

- ★ rocking, flapping, jumping
- ★ swings, jump rope, balancing boards, scooter

Proprioceptive aids

- ★ weighted blankets, lap blankets, weighted toys
- ★ compression vests, socks, body socks
- ★ compression bed sheet

Freely, authentically unmasking is a privilege, but it shouldn't be. We need to get it through our heads that human beings *need* to stim and *need* to be our authentic selves. Perhaps the greatest lesson we can learn: we need to mind our own goddamn business.

If something isn't affecting you (and I mean *really* affecting you, not the 'I'm being made to feel uncomfortable, boohoo, poor me' sort of thing), suck it up. Consider your privilege . . . or maybe go and stim for a little bit.

I don't think there's ever a moment in my life when I'm *not* stimming in some way. It's a constant for me, and something that I've learned is necessary, so I've given myself the validation and love to understand this and allow my mind and body what they need, regardless of what those around me may say or do.

I'm always wearing a piece of fidget jewellery—something that looks like normal, funky jewellery but has extra little bits and pieces that I can fiddle with and move. (Though, even if it *didn't* look like normal jewellery, who cares? My job on this Earth is not to be deemed aesthetically acceptable to the rest of the population just to make them comfortable.)

In my bag or in my pocket, I have a small square piece of *safe* fabric that I can touch and hold when I'm beginning to feel overwhelmed. I carry my noise-cancelling headphones and decibel-reducing earplugs with me everywhere. On particularly bad days, I'll take my weighted lap blanket if I need to go out. Screw anyone who looks at me oddly.

I'm a neurodivergent human, and I need extra support to get through the day in an environment that is not geared towards me. I'm not going to rid myself of that just to appease other people.

So, my dear humans: stim away.

Meltdowns

When we think of the word 'meltdown', it's often associated with toddlers throwing a temper tantrum. It's thought of as screams and fits and a face full of snot because a child didn't get their way, or due to bratty behaviour or an undisciplined child. And it's seen as a problem with the person having the meltdown—something they need to snap out of, something that is their doing, their fault and their responsibility. Meltdowns and their surrounding issues are seen as incredibly taboo for anyone older than the age of a toddler, and the older you become, the more taboo it seems to be.

Meltdowns are intense reactions to overwhelming situations. Outwardly they may manifest as screaming, crying or potentially self-harmful measures. They are involuntary coping mechanisms, and they are absolutely terrifying.

You know the static screen of a television—no signal but a loud, fuzzy, fast-moving, nonsensical picture? You know that feeling when you're between sleep and wakefulness and someone tries to talk to you—nothing makes sense and they may as well be speaking in Sims game language? They are what a meltdown feels like.

It feels like your head is imploding again, and again, and again.

It feels like you're the last human left on Earth.

It feels like your entire body is a volcanic eruption.

It feels like you're in the climax of a horror movie, and the disk is scratched so the jump scare is on repeat.

And in that moment, it feels like nothing can bring you back out of it.

Your body loses its ability to regulate, comprehend and process. We lose control of our minds, we lose control of our bodies, we lose control of our reactions to situations. And it's the most terrifying, lonely feeling in the whole world.

That is what a meltdown feels like. *That* is the truth of meltdowns.

The cause of a meltdown can change drastically, but the underlying issue is always the same. It is a neurodivergent person's reaction to trying to survive in a world that was not created for them. Meltdowns can stem from something clearly humongous: a fight, a loved one passing, a global pandemic. Or they can stem from something that, to an outsider's point of view, may seem minute: a change of plans, a lost item, a loud announcement at a train station. Sensory overload of any capacity.

The process of a meltdown is similar to the building of a wave. It may start small, beginning below the surface before there is any visible change. There is then a surge of energy that raises the ocean, even if you can't necessarily see its full force just yet.

Meltdowns are most common for me in extremely overwhelming situations that involve lots of sensory stimuli, intense emotional expectation, or even just intense emotion. There's a misconception that autistic people lack empathy, that we don't express or feel emotion, but this couldn't be further from the truth. We're a different neurotype, not a robot. Many, many autistic people process and feel emotions so deeply that even the smallest wave of emotion feels like a tsunami and can be all-encompassing, all-consuming.

Happiness feels like a fizzy drink bottle about to explode inside my tummy. Sadness feels like I'm stuck in a cave with a pool of thick molasses keeping me prisoner. My inability to cope with grief means that, after I experience a loss, I'll go emotionally numb because the idea of even thinking about or processing the grief will cause meltdowns that can last days at a time. The grief will last years, with episodes popping up constantly within that time. I still can't smell my late nanny's perfume, or hear her favourite song, or be in a room with people talking about her without spiralling into a meltdown that will last for hours, with a sick feeling in my tummy that will last for days.

Disappointment is an emotion that I'm convinced was created by a barbarian, and it is perhaps the emotion that I feel the strongest and struggle with the most. Disappointment over something as small as a drawing not coming out right, or a friend being unable to come over, or dinner being different to what Mum told me it would be can cause hours of tears. Bigger disappointments, such as missing out on tickets to a concert I was deeply looking forward to, doing badly at a horse competition or, most recently, having things I'd been excited about cancelled due to the Covid-19 pandemic, can cause hours of meltdowns and shutdowns, and depressive episodes that can last for a week. I'll fixate on the feelings of disappointment and overwhelming darkness until I can force it to make sense, fix the situation or find closure—none of which, for the most part, are attainable when it comes to situations that cause disappointment in the first place.

Meltdowns can occur during happy times, too. In fact, a big emotion of any sort can cause them. I don't think I've experienced a single Christmas Eve or birthday without a small meltdown (or sometimes a much bigger one). And sometimes, when I'm working on an acting or speaking job for weeks at a time, my entire body gives out. It's too loud, it's too bright, I haven't had enough rest. It's constant, and my stubborn arse isn't going to listen to my brain telling me that I need to stop, so my brain does it for me.

When a meltdown begins to hit me, I often begin to panic before I can even assess the situation. In that moment, fear, sadness and confusion are the only emotions in the world. Everything before or after the current situation disappears and my mind becomes hyper-focused on the way I'm feeling at that exact moment, like it's the only thing I can and ever will feel for the rest of my life. My mind abandons logic and reasoning and begins running on autopilot before

I can check the wave to see if it's tidal or merely whitewash that will smooth over. When you panic, everything looks like a tsunami.

As the wave begins to build, so does the panic and my inability for rational thinking. My breathing becomes rushed, jagged and sharp. My head becomes foggy, my teeth start to chatter. Basic comprehension and understanding of language desert me, and people's voices sound like they're coming through a funnel. Every part of my body feels too heavy and too light all at once. I'm about to crash through the ground and I'm also going to float away. I'm a volcano about to erupt, a balloon with too much air in it. I feel like Violet Beauregarde in Willy Wonka's Chocolate Factory, before they squeezed the blueberry juice out of her.

It's all too much. Too much. *Too much.*

And then comes the crashing of the wave. It's an energy that collides violently with the water beneath, resulting in a spinning, powerful force of noise and pure, negative energy. The built-up, painful energy needs to escape somehow, and in a mindset that I'm unable to comprehend and make sense of, the only way my body knows how to is by releasing it in ways that are completely involuntary. It seems entirely irrational for me to be screaming into my kneecaps as I curl up on a hard, wooden floor, piercing my skin with my fingernails or pulling out my hair, all because of a lost item, a too-loud speaker, a happy time of year with happy people . . . But it's the way it always is, isn't it?

You can't judge the intensity of a rip tide unless you yourself are in the water. And, in that moment, it's less painful for me to allow its strong current to take me than to attempt to swim out of it.

Eventually, when the triggers or emotions have dispersed and faded, the wave will settle, the rip tide will disperse, and clear waters return. But after paddling for your life for hours, it's only expected that extreme exhaustion will follow, sometimes for days at a time.

Meltdowns are not reserved for toddlers; they're an overwhelming emotional and mental collapse that autistic people of all ages will experience and continue to experience throughout their lives. Despite this, meltdowns do not *automatically* come with being autistic. There's no natural clock in our brains that alerts us: *Hey, autistic human. It's meltdown hour!* They're our brain's neurological response to situations that are harmful, scary and confusing. And, just as with rip tides, with the right information, understanding and support, we can learn to avoid them and overcome them.

I'm an adult woman, and meltdowns are still a part of my life; they likely always will be, unless we can magically, overnight create a society that suits me perfectly. However, I've learned to lean on the support of my people, avoid putting excess pressure on myself and spot my own warning signs.

SIGNS OF AN IMPENDING MELTDOWN

- ★ increased irritability
- ★ increased stimming
- ★ change in voice
- ★ lack of communication abilities
- ★ anxiety
- ★ freezing
- ★ loss of ability to focus
- ★ changes in body language.

WHEN YOUR CHILD IS HAVING A MELTDOWN

Meltdowns are not tantrums

Tantrums are wilful, goal-oriented outbursts of frustration, while meltdowns are the result of overstimulating situations creating overwhelming feelings. They are the result of our brains being exposed to too much for too long. Reacting to a meltdown the same way you would a tantrum is not helpful and could cause more harm and stress.

Be empathetic and understanding

Your child is going through emotional and physical pain that is almost unimaginable unless you have been there yourself. They're struggling to process and understand, and the best thing you can do is to be there for your child in whatever way they need. Give them space, give them time, give them understanding. Meltdowns are scary, confusing and embarrassing, and the last thing in the world they need is the person who is supposed to support and love them unconditionally making them out to be a nuisance.

Understand the wave that your child is in

When an autistic person is so lost in their emotions, the wave may be so loud that we're unable to hear anything except for the roaring of it. Rationality and processing is not high on your child's priority list now, and coming at them with rationality, reason and logic may as well be an alien language. What you can do is let them know that they are safe and loved. Reassure them that you are near, that they're in a safe place and that you're ready to repair the boat once the storm stops.

→

Never punish or shame a meltdown

Meltdowns are entirely out of your child's control, so being punished, ridiculed and resented will only lead to them feeling more isolated, anxious and fearful. Do not tell them to go to their room, to 'snap out of it' or react with anger and shame-filled remarks. Allow your child the space and freedom to feel, to cry, to simply be, and let them know that they're supported.

In public meltdowns, focus on your child

Public meltdowns often cause the most embarrassment and fear for both the child and the parents. Don't let your reaction be influenced by the stares of bystanders or any internal dialogue that your child needs to be disciplined. It is crucial to focus on your child and make them your top priority; they are struggling and need your support. Ensure that they are safe both physically and emotionally.

Don't. Film. Your. Kids.

Don't make them feel like zoo animals, or more exposed than they're already undoubtedly feeling. If your child is experiencing intense emotional and physical pain, stress and trauma and your first thought is to take out your phone, video them and post it to your Facebook page with *#autismmamalife* and *God gives the hardest battles to the strongest humans <3 xoxo*, with the false impression that it's for 'education' or 'awareness' purposes, think again. I have the legal obligation to hunt you down for sport.

Shutdowns

Shutdowns are caused by the same struggles that cause meltdowns: sensory overload, high levels of stress and an inability to cope with a situation any longer. And, much like a meltdown, a shutdown presents itself internally in the same ways that a wave builds, or the static noise on a television. The difference between the two is the way they present themselves externally.

Meltdowns feel and look like a volcano about to erupt, while shutdowns feel and look like a tortoise recoiling into their shell, or a toy car's battery beginning to die. Often, a shutdown will follow on from a meltdown.

During a meltdown, the stress chemicals in our brain reach boiling point, causing us to lash out explosively. During a shutdown, the nervous system becomes overwhelmed and shuts down to protect itself. Shutdowns are less obvious, more internalised and very often go unnoticed.

SIGNS OF A SHUTDOWN

- ★ zoning out
- ★ forgetting simple tasks
- ★ withdrawing to a quiet, dark space
- ★ lying down on flat surfaces
- ★ becoming completely still
- ★ complete silence
- ★ not communicating with friends (including via text).

Like meltdowns, shutdowns are extremely taxing and can take days or weeks to recover from. Learn your signs, learn what helps you to best recover, and honour your mind and body enough to give yourself what you need.

HOW TO SUPPORT YOURSELF OR SOMEONE ELSE IN SHUTDOWN

Learn the triggers

Much like meltdowns, shutdowns are triggered by an intense emotional response to an overwhelming situation. Each person will have their own triggers, signs and causes. Once you understand both what can trigger a shutdown, and what the individual signs are, learning to avoid and manage them becomes easier.

Remove yourself from the situation

Removing yourself from the situation is vital. Seek out a safe, quiet place to be alone (or with a person you feel safe with, as being alone during a shutdown can cause the situation to become even scarier). If you're at home, this may be your bedroom. If you're out, find a quiet place away from any crowds where you can safely sit down.

Keep communication simple

Simple 'yes or no' questions, hand signals, or communication cards can be beneficial when audible and verbal communication becomes too tough, as is often the case during a shutdown. Reduce interaction to only what is necessary to stay safe.

Eliminate expectation, demand and responsibility

A shutdown is quite literally that—the brain shutting down to cope with what is happening. And, like the rainbow-buffering cursor on a computer, it cannot simply be stopped. The person needs time to recover so push aside expectations and demands and allow them that time.

Ask the autistic person before a shutdown happens

If there are signs that a shutdown may be imminent, ask the person *before* shutdown happens how best to assist them. While the psychological response is the same, shutdowns look different for every person and, as a result, their needs may vary.

If your child is in shutdown

See the tips for meltdowns, on pages 61–62. These all apply to shutdowns as well.

Burnout

Living in a society built for neurotypical humans—something I am not and can never be—means that my body and my mind have to work overtime, just to survive.

Meltdowns, shutdowns or sensory overload are only short-term events. But burnout is the end result of long-term exposure to expectations and pressures that are a mismatch to ability and, without adequate support, can last for months. Burnout often shows itself in neurodivergent people as a loss of function and skills, chronic exhaustion and reduced tolerance to sensory stimuli.

Because of both the intensity of burnout and its long time frame, burnout can cause people to lose jobs, drop out of school and dramatically alter their lives. Despite all of this, burnout seems to be one of the least spoken about and least understood parts of autism, meaning that services, support and correct understanding are few and far between. And, once again, autistic folk are left to try and figure it all out themselves.

Autistic people experience two types of burnout: 'social burnout' and 'autistic burnout'.

Social burnout happens all too frequently, when just surviving in a neurotypical world causes you to collapse with exhaustion at the end of the day. Every single day, neurodivergent people are forced to live in ways that go against everything we see as accurate and achievable. We're forced to communicate in ways that are different, to follow schedules that don't fit our minds, and are fed constant sensory stimuli that is too loud, too bright, *too much*.

As a survival method, many of us will put on a mask so as not to be called out, ostracised or left behind. But, while the mask serves its purpose to help us fit into society, it ultimately becomes our demise. We become exhausted to the point where our brain has to go on autopilot and shut itself down to protect us.

But, *what is* burnout?

You know when you have too many tabs open on your computer and the computer freezes up or starts to slow down or go into 'safe mode'—*that's it*. Our brains start working on limited functions, not all services available, because we've been giving far too much of our services for far too long.

Except, the difference between our brains and computers is that on a safe-mode computer screen, we can physically see the rainbow-loading circle, we can see the slower functioning time and understand why it's happening. As an autistic person? We're not given that privilege.

As an autistic person, we are expected to function, to go on with our lives, to carry on and repeat the exact same behaviours that got us into this rainbow-loading screen in the first place because 'everyone else can—so suck it up'. And we'll fall. And we'll crash. And we'll keep on crashing. We'll crash again, and again, and again as we're forced into these scenarios to be washed, rinsed, repeated and spat back out again.

Until we can't anymore.

Our bodies can only take so much, and after too long of too much, we can't continue anymore. We go into safe mode.

Autistic burnout can last for weeks, months or even years. And it's one of the most terrifying things you can experience. For long periods of time, we're unable to put on the mask that we've worked for years to perfect. While the idea of that sounds absolutely lovely (we've all lived through Covid-19, nothing beats that 'taking your mask off' feeling), it's something that can become dangerous and debilitating when it's done because of burnout, especially in a society that demonises people who act in ways different to the expected.

Our ability to communicate may fade away.

Our ability to regulate and express emotions may disintegrate.

We lose basic abilities and seem to regress.

Finding reason and motivation may as well be a trip to the moon, and our lives can become dark, loud and scary.

Burnout is something that isn't much spoken about outside of the autistic community, but it's something that we desperately need to shine a light on. Masking and an inability to fit into society's expectations have a direct connection to suicide rates, with autistic people more than ten times more likely than non-autistic people to die by suicide, and autistic women being particularly at risk.

As with everything else in this chapter (minus stimming), burnout isn't an inherent part of being autistic. It's not something that *has* to come with the territory. It's something that happens to autistic people because of the world we live in.

We need to create a more understanding world, a world where societal expectations don't begin and end at the neurotypical, capitalised standard, a world where workplaces and schools gear their schedules, requirements and understandings towards a wider range of people than those who seem to fit the social norms. A world where neurodivergent people are openly *allowed* to be neurodivergent.

We need to create a more understanding world . . . A world where neurodivergent people are openly *allowed* to be neurodivergent.

A world where masking isn't an expectation, but 'coming as you are' is.

Until then, here are some things we can do to minimise burnout, and to care for ourselves or others when it inevitably happens.

SIGNS OF BURNOUT

- ★ constant fatigue
- ★ increased irritability
- ★ increased anxiety
- ★ increased or decreased sensitivity to sensory stimuli
- ★ loss of speech
- ★ reduced memory capacity (forgetfulness, memory loss, brain fog)
- ★ inability to effectively communicate
- ★ decrease in motivation
- ★ several meltdowns/shutdowns over a short period of time
- ★ loss of executive functioning abilities
- ★ unable to maintain 'social masks' or use social skills
- ★ difficulty with self-care (showering, eating, brushing teeth, getting dressed, exercising)
- ★ seeming 'more autistic'.

HOW TO PROTECT YOURSELF DURING BURNOUT

Rest

Your body is screaming at you to rest and it is vital that you look after yourself and do exactly that. Schedule time to do absolutely nothing. Use the tools that most benefit you, and allow yourself the freedom to do nothing other than care for yourself. The world will keep spinning, I promise you.

Take all the time you need to recover

You are not a robot. You are a neurodivergent human doing your best and you do not owe your existence to anyone. Give yourself the time you need to recover or you'll end up in a continuous cycle of burnout.

Allow yourself to be autistic

Spoiler alert: if you're a neurodivergent human, you're allowed to be neurodivergent. Stim, you beautiful human. Stimming is a vital self-regulatory behaviour, and something we need to do in order to function and stave off burnout.

Keep socialising to a minimum

For many of us, socialising can be a huge overload. Keep social gatherings to a minimum, or just with those people with whom you feel the safest, and learn to say no if you're not up to something.

Rely on your social network

Humans are social creatures who rely on each other for survival. Just as we don't call a flower weak for needing the sun to grow, or the ocean weak for needing the moon to pull and push the tides, we are not weak for needing each other. Allow your loved ones and those around you to support you.

Minimise your expectations

You don't have to take on the world. If you finish your day by eating something, drinking water and brushing your teeth, consider it a win.

HOW TO AVOID BURNOUT

★ schedule breaks
★ reduce expectations

- voice your needs to your teachers, boss and loved ones
- learn to unmask and factor in times to do so
- recognise your personal burnout signs
- prioritise your to-do list (When I wake up, I assess what sort of day I'm having. If it's a good day, I'll create a normal to-do list and highlight a few key things that need to be completed; the rest are just a bonus. On days that aren't so good, I highlight only one 'must do' and make sure the rest of the day is used for self-care. This 'must do' may be as simple as 'go for a walk', or 'change bed sheets'.)
- learn to say no
- find time for self-care ('Cutesy' self-care and practical self-care both have parts to play. Have that bubble bath, put on that face mask, watch that comfort show, but also eat, shower and drink water.)
- factor recovery time into your daily routine; make it mandatory.

Meltdowns, shutdowns and burnouts are all parts of being autistic that are close to inevitable. Despite not being inherent parts of being neurodivergent, they're the result of having a neurotype that is not supported by the world we're living in. In a dream world, we will no longer have to experience them because our social systems will be entirely accepting, understanding, supportive and accommodating of different neurotypes. However, at this point, a world like that is akin to a One Direction reunion . . . pretty unlikely.

Until then, we can create a more nurturing environment by surrounding ourselves with love and support, learning and becoming friends with our minds, and continuing to dismantle harmful social norms in ourselves and in our networks.

CHAPTER 4

Friends and Sidekicks

I think perhaps my favourite part of every Disney fairytale isn't necessarily the Happily Ever After. It's not the seemingly spontaneous songs that appear out of nowhere, or the moment when the princess gets her prince, or the land of make-believe that you can lose yourself in. It is the part when every single Disney fairytale hero or heroine, after the beginning stages of doom, gloom and despair, finds themselves in their Adventure stage. This is when they meet and battle their dragons, when they have to walk through the valley of darkness or the mouth of an anthropomorphised tiger cave. The Adventure stage is also when we meet our sidekicks.

That is my favourite part. The fact that even in the scariest moments, they *always* find their sidekicks.

Think back to your favourite Disney movie, your favourite cliché 'good guy versus bad guy', 'once upon a time to happily ever after' story. Was there a sidekick?

In *The Lion King*, after his father's horrendously dramatic death by an absolute satanic uncle with a heart made of pure stone, Simba is thrown from Pride Rock and told never to return. The little lion cub has lost his dad, his family, everything he knows, and it seems the fairytale will end there. How else can an abandoned, hungry, dehydrated baby's story end? But lo and behold, we're then introduced to two loveable, crazy, outcast, definitely ADHD-coded creatures who come into the picture when Simba needs them most. They're more than a bit peculiar, but they see Simba and realise that they've been pushed into a new chapter, that suddenly the pages of their own stories have turned.

After meeting Simba, these two could have chosen to do one of three things:

1. They could have left him. This would have been fair. After all, declining to adopt the most ferocious carnivore in Africa would have been a reasonable choice.

2. They could have recognised him for who he was and forced him to become king before he was ready. Again, fair and reasonable. Climb up the food chain, baby. Make friends with the predator.
3. They could have taken him in and loved him for who he was at that point of his life—without question, without vacillation, with absolute irrefutability.

They, of course, chose the third option. And, because of them, Simba's story can continue.

In *Aladdin*, Genie has been a prisoner for ten thousand years. Feeling defeated, he has begun to accept that this is all his life will ever be. A prisoner. Trapped. Tethered for eternity to a magic lamp, at the beckoning call of whoever may pick it up. Until, a homeless street rat who struggles to simply survive comes along and makes a promise. He isn't going to let Genie be alone. Because of Aladdin, for the first time in Genie's life, he has hope.

In *The Hunchback of Notre Dame* we meet Esmeralda, a beautiful Romani woman, who is the only one in the entire world to show Quasimodo kindness—perhaps because she feels the same way as him: rejected by society. As she wanders through the church, she sings 'God Help the Outcasts', one of the best musical pieces of modern-day history. A song that, due to copyright reasons, I am unable to include the lyrics for within these pages, but I deeply urge you to go google them. Right now. Go.

Now, I know that I have a tendency to become overly, unnaturally, unhealthily obsessed over things—I have ADHD; it's part of the contract—but from a young age this song became a huge part of my identity. My oxygen intake came from this song, my source of life came from this song . . . my reason for being was this song.

Little me—selectively mute, terrified of the world—would unashamedly scream this song at the top of my lungs with tears pouring down my cheeks and snot coming out of both nostrils, belting the lyrics like an autistic banshee, as if these words had been written just for me. (On one occasion, I stood on top of a table at a La Porchetta restaurant and sang it. The surprised waitress gave me a free vanilla ice-cream cone. My first paying gig. *Nice.*) However, it wasn't until I was eighteen that I suddenly realised why this song meant so much to me: *I* was the outcast that Esmeralda sings about.

I was that outcast, and all I wanted in the whole world was for one person to look at me the same way Esmeralda looks at Quasimodo. I longed for one person to see past what society told me I was, or what I never would be, and to see me, as me. I needed someone to look past my metaphorical hunched back, just as Esmeralda does for Quasimodo, and to see me for the human that I was, not the expectation that I could never be.

And yes, okay. I had my parents, something I will always be incredibly grateful for. But growing up you need more than someone who's, like, mentally programmed to love you. You need your tribe, your people, your sidekicks, and I didn't have them. I was the lion cub in the desert, the trapped Genie, the hidden-away Quasimodo, but I was without a sidekick to bring me through the middle chapters of my story.

The impossibility of making friends

In my Once Upon a Time, when everyone else was well and truly making friends, socialising—you know, doing the whole 'person' thing—I hadn't at all figured out what I was supposed to do. *Friendships? Conversations? Socialising? Sorry, come again?*

The mere act of igniting friendship was not only an alien concept to me, but also one that had backfired immensely. After

I longed for one person
to see past what society
told me I was,
or what I never would be,
and to see me, as me.

many, many, *many* failed attempts, my parents—being the loving people they are and acknowledging the struggle I was having with fitting in—did what any overly supportive parent would do to help their daughter spark friendships: buy them. *Absolutely stellar.*

In primary school, after I'd struggled all year to fit in and make friends (probably a curse for blowing out Jesus, honestly), my parents decided to give a bit of a helping hand and throw the biggest, heck-of-a-sized Christmas party that the world had ever seen, inviting every child in my class and bribing them into coming with promises of Santa and monstrous amounts of party food, games and presents.

Of course, everyone RSVP'd, and thirty children rocked up with their best party clothes on, the brightest of smiles and friendly conversation. It was the party of my dreams, the party of the millennium, and every child in my class was eager and ready to befriend me. In that moment, I wholeheartedly *embodied* the 'it girl'. I *was* the main character.

No more awkward interactions or lonely, sad schooldays for me. No more broken amber necklaces or discarded pandas (though, just for safekeeping, I had hidden my precious items in my parents' locked bedroom). Five-year-old me naively thought that this sudden bout of friendship was all my own doing. I had finally, mysteriously mastered the art of making friends. Now, however, I realise the promise of presents maybe had something to do with it. *Ignorance is bliss,* or whatever they say, and for a few hours, I was the happiest that I think I had ever been.

But blissful ignorance can only last so long. The following day, I went to school, absolutely on top of the world and genuinely expecting to be greeted with the same bright smiles and open arms. That day, I got taken to the basketball court and beaten up.

Another time, when I was turning ten, there were a few girls at school I thought I was close with, and I told Mum that I would like to invite them to my birthday party. Mum, eager about the idea of her daughter trying to make friends again (and quite possibly knowing something that I didn't), prompted me against the idea of a little party and instead, in typical *my family* style, went all out.

In order to convince these girls to come, a stretch limousine was hired to pick them up from their homes and take us to the biggest shopping complex in my state, where we went on a huge shopping spree, and got matching Build-A-Bears and 'BFF' necklaces. We went out for a fancy dinner and came back to my place where the best slumber party Australia had ever seen was waiting for us.

As I sat watching *Flicka* with my new group of best friends (I knew they were, because we had the necklaces to prove it), my body tingled with excitement. I'd done it. I had best friends. It had taken me ten years, but heck, I had done it.

The following day, I went to school wearing my BFF necklace and was over the moon to find the other girls wearing theirs, too. But as it turned out, the only reason they were wearing their necklaces was so they could take them off in front of me, throw them in the rubbish bin and proudly tell me, 'We would never be friends with you'. A note was offered to me that same day from one of the girls, very politely telling me that all of them would rather if we pretended the party hadn't happened as they didn't want to be seen with me at school. She signed it off with a *XX*, so that was nice, I suppose.

At the beginning of high school, my school thought it would be a brilliant idea for all of us to go on a big camp to get to know each other. Reluctantly, and with a lot of tears, I had given in to my parents' pleas and agreed to go. The camp itself was fine; I even managed to make friends with a girl I once again convinced myself would be a lifelong best friend. However, come the first week of school, she bluetoothed me a 'diss track' she had written about me (in her defence, it was by far the most creative method of disowning me I've ever received), broke into my locker and scribbled slurs on all of my notebooks, and began spreading rumours about me that caused the teachers to call me into uncomfortable, worried meetings. Those rumours stayed with me long after I left the school. (Just so you're aware, I'm now a proud mother of three children, all while doing seances and witchcraft in the science room.)

Whatever best friends I made through my teenage years ditched me because, 'My mum said I might turn out like you, and I'm scared about that happening ... sorry', or 'My other friends tease me for having an autistic best friend. It's just too stressful on my mental health. But tell your little sister she's still invited to my birthday party!'

Time and time again, I learned just how seemingly impossible it was for me to form any sort of friendship, and how alien the entire process was to me. It was like learning a new language, but the rules kept on changing every single day. *Nothing* made sense. *Nothing* worked. And no matter how hard I tried, I just couldn't get the hang of it or figure it out. I could never make friends, nor figure out who the right people were to make friends with. People were strange, weird and confusing, and the more I did to try and fit in and understand them, the more it backfired right in my face. Clearly, friendship was not a thing that came naturally, easily or kindly to me—nor does it for many neurodivergent people.

What is friendship?

Friendship is a concept that is often built on a foundation that doesn't have any clear rules, laws or suggestions. It doesn't make sense, and the rules change daily, minutely and situationally. With blokes, my understanding is that if they find a common interest in kicking a footy, or sharing a joke, or something that's independent of deeper, unspoken communication, then everything's handy-dandy. Their friendships don't have to be built on intense emotional connection and social skills.

But when it comes to female friendships, my experience is that the relationship is almost entirely built on communication, talking and societal expectations that have to be met—skills neurodivergent girls often lack. There are so many hidden and unspoken rules, and it's incredibly difficult, even for those who may not be neurodivergent.

Most of our communication is non-verbal, and that fact is often entirely missed by autistic folk. It shows up as eye contact, body language, tone, gestures, posture ... the list goes on. And we're expected to understand, maintain and use that 93 per cent of communication—meaning that, when we don't, not only can we become incredibly confused but our actions and reactions can also then be misconstrued by those around us.

We are expected to socialise in the same way that our neurotypical peers do, despite our brains being anything but. And, while many typical folk share common perceptions of the world, friendship and communication and can easily pick up on non-verbal cues, the thought of all that may seem almost alien to someone who's neurodivergent. This leads us to becoming outcast, bullied and led astray. Forty-three per cent of autistic teenagers never interact with peers outside of school, 54 per cent of them have never received phone calls, texts or unplanned communication, and 50 per cent have never been invited to a party or activity. We're left without sidekicks, without people to call our own. The school years, when communication is forced upon us, are without a doubt the hardest.

Friendship doesn't come easily to a lot of us. We simply can't see peers our own age and spark friendships with them solely because we were born in the same year and the universe happened to drop us on the same part of Earth. We need *our* people, *our* tribe. We need people to fill up the middle section of our fairytale. Our sidekicks.

School might not be the place where many neurodivergent children will find their tribe, but that doesn't mean they aren't out there. In fact, we have the ability to find the most beautiful sidekicks. At our own time, in our own place.

Finding friends . . . my way

When I left school and was given the opportunity to step out and engage with the world at my own pace, that's when I started to discover my people. Originally, my people came in the form of internet-based friendships. (I know, I know. *Internet danger! Stranger danger! Stay in the real world!*) These internet friendships were with complete and utter strangers—I knew nothing about them but their screen names—but they were my first massive step towards learning both how to communicate and how to find myself. In my social groups online, I wasn't 'Chloé, the weird autistic girl with knotty brown hair and flappy hands', I was 'Chloé, the artist, the blogger, the writer, the one who knows absolutely everything about One Direction and can eagerly blab to everyone else because we all came here for that sole purpose'.

There were no expectations that I couldn't meet, no false ideologies that had been put in place, no need to force communication, no fear of having to make eye contact. And despite never having met these people in person, never having heard their voices or even seen many of their faces, these friendships were more meaningful and impactful than any of the 'real life' relationships I had ever built.

Once I started to feel more comfortable in my own skin, I started to step out further, and began to find friendship in the most beautiful places. *My* places.

I found friendship in my weekly horse-riding lessons, because all we would do is sit in the stables and talk about ponies.

I found friendship in the community theatre, because together we created beautiful plays and musicals (and all of my lines had already been chosen for me).

I found friendship with surfers at the beach, because there was no need to talk. We'd just listen to the waves and cheer each other on as we caught them and rode them in.

I found friendship in groups specifically catering to other autistic people, where my flappy hands and excited rambles and lack of eye contact was mirrored—many of these people have become lifelong friends.

I found friendships when I was no longer forced into communicating the way the world wanted me to; instead, I was allowed to simply be me.

After Simba has a clown of a warthog, a sassy meerkat and an enthusiastic old monkey to show him that he is worth so much more than the impression he'd been left with in his darkest moment, he finds the courage, strength and motivation to go back to Pride Rock and become the King of all Africa.

Because of a kind homeless boy, the loud, crazy Genie gets his number one wish and becomes free, no longer a prisoner.

After twenty years of being hidden away from society, the city accepts Quasimodo for who he is, just as Esmeralda did. Because of the love they show him, he's able to find that same love within himself. He's different, but he's accepted. Not just by the city but, most importantly, by himself.

In those moments, I like to imagine how the sidekick characters were feeling. Can you imagine how Timon and Pumbaa felt when they saw Simba standing on top of Pride Rock, knowing they were the ones who helped him get to his Happily Ever After? Or how Aladdin felt after he saw the Genie's chains break, knowing a ten-thousand-year curse had been lifted?

These sidekicks are the most important characters in any person's story. If I had had an Esmeralda, a Timon and Pumbaa or an Aladdin, my Once Upon a Time might not have been quite so far from my Happily Ever After.

If one peer in primary school had asked, 'Hey, do you want to hang out with us?'

If one friend had said, 'I know times are tough, but I'm here with you.'

If one teacher had reassured me with, 'I promise, I won't let you do this alone.'

Your sidekicks are out there

Maybe you're reading this thinking, *It is a brilliant life lesson for somebody else but not for me, because how on earth does a girl I don't know and her silly metaphors with an excessive use of Disney stories apply to me?*

Here's how: we are all living in a fairytale.

Every single one of us has our own story, with our own Once Upon a Times, our own Adventure stages, our own Happily Ever Afters. And just like all fairytales, each of our stories also includes the sidekicks, the sidekicks' sidekicks and the villains.

In your story, you're the main character. You're the hero. (It's only fair, we all deserve our main character moment.) But who are you in someone else's story? What part are you going to play? Are you going to be the sidekick? Are you going to be the person who helps someone else's story continue, just by being there? By showing kindness, by showing understanding? Are you going to be the sidekick's sidekick, just as Timon and Pumbaa had the lionesses, and Aladdin had Jasmine and Abu, and Esmeralda eventually had the entire town?

We are all living in a fairytale, and you need to choose who you will play. Because if you don't actively choose your part, someone else is going to pick it for you . . . and there is every chance that you may be the villain.

Every single one of us has the ability to be someone's sidekick, not in spite of our own differences, but because of them. Aladdin was a street rat, Esmeralda was an outcast, Timon and Pumbaa were absolute oddities. Sidekicks come from incredibly diverse backgrounds; it's because of their differences that they are able to create change and have a significant impact. We all have the ability to create change. We all have the ability to be someone's sidekick.

Society puts massive importance on the idea of 'best friends', the idea that there is one singular human who will be there for you through everything, who understands every fibre of your soul, you never once tire of and you adore unconditionally. But *best friends* aren't important. What *is* important is having good people in your life.

I still don't have one person in my life I would consider my 'best friend'. I don't mention this in a sad, 'woe and pity me' sort of a way, but in a comfortable 'this is how my story works best' way. It's something that I've not only come to comfortable terms with, but also became content with. It's a keystone of my story.

I don't have one be-all person, but I have a group of good, kind, wonderful people who have become parts of my story.

Every single one of us has the ability to be someone's sidekick, not in spite of our own differences, but because of them.

I have the sixty-year-old cowboys, who in another life I may never even have considered talking with, but when we're sitting around a campfire at a rodeo, or cheering each other on from the arena sidelines, in that moment, those people are *my* people.

I have friends I met while lining up for our favourite singer. We became good friends immediately after asking, 'What's your favourite song?' and for the rest of the night, those people were and still are *my* people. (So much so, in fact, that I have matching tattoos with three of the people I met in line.)

I have the friends I met online. I have never met them in person but those people are *my* people.

I have a rich, full, beautiful fairytale filled with my people, because after far too long, and far too much heartbreak, broken necklaces and promises, I've discovered that I deserve good people—and so do you.

We deserve people who make us feel like we're our best self when we're simply being ourselves.

We deserve people who love us, and support us, and don't try to change us—just as Esmeralda didn't try to change Quasi.

We deserve people. Good people.

And I intend to keep mine.

HOW TO FIND YOUR TRIBE

Your people, your friends, your sidekicks are out there; you just need to find them.

Join social groups

What are your hobbies? What makes you tick? What makes your eyes sparkle? Find social groups where you're going to be surrounded by like-minded people. This could be a club at your school, or a sports team, a community group, a volunteer organisation, a local theatre company or even an online forum—online friendships can be just as meaningful as in-person friendships, and can often be an easier place to start. Seek out your local and online communities to find ones that click with you. It's so much easier to make friends and find your people when you're all there for a common reason.

Don't settle

It can be so easy to accept whoever comes your way, especially if friendship isn't something that comes easily to you. But walking a path alone for a while longer is better than sharing it with someone who's going to make that path more difficult. Don't settle for people who are unkind to you, who force you to conform, who don't care for your true, authentic self.

Define your own friendship goals

Society puts a lot of importance on the idea that we have to have a large social network, and that social success is lots of friends, but that couldn't be further from the truth. Whether friendship for you comes in the form of a few close friends, or more people you only speak to for certain social groups, or online friends—you're the only one who can define what friendship means for you.

Most importantly: be yourself

You are the only you there is, and that is the most beautiful thing in the whole world. Contorting, conforming and masking yourself into being someone you are not will only lead to long-term harm. Be you, because *your* people are out there. The people who will love *you* unconditionally for all that *you* are. If you need to hide yourself to be accepted by someone else, that person is not your person.

FOR SIDEKICKS: HOW TO SUPPORT YOUR NEURODIVERGENT FRIENDS

Here are some ways you can support your neurodivergent friends.

Make an effort to understand their neurodiversity

No one's asking you to become a human Wikipedia and know absolutely every tiny detail about the neurodivergent brain. I've been neurodivergent my entire life and I still don't understand how my brain works most days. But our brains are wired differently, and making an effort to understand that is going to benefit both parties. While that can mean doing research beforehand (if you're reading this book right now, *solid* start), it mainly means talking to the individual and asking what they need for support.

For anyone, these six words can make a world of difference: 'How can I best support you?'

Make plans (and be sure to include them!)

There's a misconception that autistic people don't *want* to make friends and that we prefer to be by ourselves. Autistic folk are frequently left out of birthday parties and social events and, while this can be due to genuine, purposeful exclusion to avoid bullying and nasty behaviour, it can at times be because of this misunderstanding around autism.

> 'Oh, we won't invite her out for after-work drinks, she doesn't like that sort of stuff.'
> 'He never wants to come anyway.'
> 'They don't like social gaths.'

Here's a top tip: while perhaps *yes,* the invitation to go out somewhere that could potentially be a sensory nightmare won't be accepted all of the time, the invitation is still very much wanted.

That way, we know we're the ones who declined an invitation, rather than never being invited in the first place. It puts it into our hands and our control.

Communicate clearly

Language is confusing; people are confusing. With 93 per cent of communication being non-verbal, and many autistic people struggling with that 93 per cent, we are at times only taking in 7 per cent of what's being communicated.

We're not always going to process what you're saying in the way that you might assume it was communicated, so by speaking literally (instead of using metaphors), speaking clearly, and allowing us time to process and take in information, it's going to make both parties a lot better off, a lot less confused and a lot happier!

The other part of communication is communicating your own feelings. Friendship is a two-way street; it's mutual. Be honest about your needs and your feelings at all times, with no exceptions. If you're not articulating your feelings, we're not going to pick up on it—we don't take hints, we don't pick up on invisible social cues, we're not going to understand radio silence. We need real communication or we're both going to get confused and upset.

If you want us there to support you for something, tell us.

If we're acting in a way you don't like, tell us.

Don't be scared of honesty; that's the key to friendship on both sides.

All parties involved deserve to feel safe, loved, respected and accepted.

Respect our sensory and social differences

The world can be a really big, really scary, really overwhelming place and sometimes we need that extra space, that extra time alone, to recalibrate and get ourselves in the right mindset to get back into the world.

Because of sensory processing disorder, sometimes things that are deemed as normal and acceptable within social settings (a hug, a handshake, a squeal) can feel like we are single-handedly being slaughtered as a human sacrifice. Just because we may not want a hug, or we can't attend your favourite concert, or we need a day of not communicating at all, it doesn't mean we don't love and value you. It simply means that we're processing the world in our own way. It's important for you to accept and understand that these needs are important for us, and it doesn't reflect on you or our friendship.

Don't treat your neurodivergent friends like a project

I hate that this is something that actually needs to be said, but it has happened enough times that it needs to be brought to attention.

I had a friend once who used her friendship with me as a crutch. She would tell everyone who would listen that she was 'friends with someone with autism', like she was the second coming of Mary Magdalene herself, like the mere existence of a friendship with someone like me was the greatest sacrifice.

We have spent our entire lives being coddled and ostracised and told we're not what we can be just because we're neurodivergent. We don't need community-service friendships. We are not charity projects.

If you have a friend who's neurodivergent and you leave them out of events, bring up their diagnosis because it's a quirky little clout chaser, don't speak to them the same way you speak to your neurotypical friends, then maybe you're not friends with them for the right reasons.

Treat us the same way you would treat any of your other mates.

At the end of the day, yes, we're different. And yes, our minds work differently. And yes, we communicate differently. And yes, you need to be understanding and lenient (although, if you're not doing this already with all of your mates . . . baby, I don't know what to tell you).

But, overall, we're one and the same. We're all humans, we all yearn for friendship and companionship. All friendship should be mutually beneficial and built on kindness and respect.

CHAPTER 5

Mental Health

Note: throughout this chapter, I'll be discussing sexual abuse, eating disorders, anxiety, depression, mental health and suicide. If these topics are sensitive for you, please respect yourself and your mind enough to step away, take a breath or skip the parts that may cause panic or worry. Your triggers are valid, your mind is valid. Please respect your mind and what it needs to turn away from or speak to someone you trust if things are too uncomfortable.

Look for this content warning symbol ⚠ *before each potential trigger and avoid that specific content if you so choose.*

When we think of the term 'mental health', our minds tend to go to the extremities of *poor* mental health, as if mental health is inherently a bad, negative, scary thing. We might think of worst-case scenarios, of stigmas that Hollywood, the media and more broadly society have taught us to associate with the term.

If I ask you to think of a film in which the lead character experiences 'mental health', how many of you immediately think of *The Joker* or *Split*? How many of you immediately correlate mental health with movies based on fear and thrillers? And, likewise, when I ask you to think of words that correlate with the term 'mental health', which ones immediately come to mind? Are they positive or negative words?

Stop for a moment and think.

What is mental health?

I used to work in the mental health sector within high schools, and when I asked students to tell me what words came to mind when they thought about mental health, they usually said things such as 'bad', 'depression', 'insane', 'self-harm' and 'suicide'. I never once asked them to describe *poor* mental health, or a mental illness. And yet, this is what they gave me. This is what many of us think.

Negative. Scary. Bad.

Our global societal understanding of mental health has led us to be fearful of it, fearful of poor mental health, and to associate mental health and its surrounding language with specific groups. We (as a community) think only some people experience poor mental health, that only specific groups have valid reasons for being mentally unwell, and those of us who do experience poor mental health but aren't in these target groups are invalidated, wrong, hypochondriacs or dramatic.

This societal mindset has given us the wrong impression—that it is wrong to experience poor mental health and to judge (albeit, often subconsciously) those who are struggling with it. This is particularly so for young people, who hear from elders and peers that they have no right to feel the way they do because they are young, have no worries, don't have anything big enough in their life to allow them to be mentally ill.

'You have a good family, you shouldn't be sad.'

'You're so pretty, you're not allowed to feel badly about your appearance.'

'Other people have it worse than you.'

'You're too young to be depressed.'

'It's because you're on that phone all day.'

'You think it's hard now? Just wait until you're older.'

'Just because that TikToker said so, doesn't mean it's true.'

We've been taught these thoughts and ideas by older generations and a global ideology based on false narratives of what mental health is.

Mental health is not innately bad or innately good; it simply *is*. Our mental health, just like our physical health, is something that is present within all of us, every day. It's a part of our constant, it's a part of our always. You always have mental health, just as you always have physical health.

When you're experiencing happiness, that's mental health. When you're experiencing sadness, that's mental health. When you're calm, when you're nervous ... it's all mental health. And, just like our physical health, it is vital that we look after it—and not just when it becomes bad. Still, we only tend to discuss mental health when we are in the pits, and in ways that are seen as taboo and weird and hidden, despite the fact that mental health is always part of us.

⚠ Suicide, mental illness

Having said that, more than 50 per cent of people will struggle with a serious mental illness at some point in our lives. Of course, this statistic only gets worse among those of us who have grown up disabled or neurodivergent. Seventy-two per cent of autistic people also struggle with a comorbid mental illness, and disabled people as a whole are five times more likely to struggle with mental illness than able-bodied, neurotypical folk. Worst of all, disabled people are dying by suicide at five times the rate of their non-disabled counterparts, and autistic people are more likely to die by suicide.

This is *why* discussing mental health—all aspects of mental health—is so deeply important. This is *why*, despite this chapter being the hardest for me to write, it is the chapter I deem the most important.

I've never been one for being silent, and I've never been one for listening to what society tells me to be silent about ... So, here's my mental health story.

Our mental health, just like our physical health, is something that is present within all of us, every day.

My Once Upon a Time

⚠ Sexual assault, PTSD

Even before neurotypical expectations had deeply sunk their claws into me, at the ripe old age of seven I was diagnosed with post-traumatic stress disorder (PTSD), something that is expected to present in older men and war veterans, not seven-year-old little girls.

This is a part of my story that I promised myself I would never bring up, that I wanted to bury so deep in my soul that nothing could ever bring it to the surface—even now, my tummy is turning, and my hands are shaking on the keyboard as I type. I've had to take multiple breaks and long walks as I write this down, and I've had to speak to my therapist, my mum and my partner multiple times so their calm, steady voices could pull me out of what could become a pit of despair that I may not crawl out of. But it is a story that, after a lot of talking, a lot of prayer and a lot of consideration, I'm ready to share.

Call me an optimist, or religious, or delusional, but I think when bad things happen to us it opens a door of opportunity to help other people. Of course, this doesn't take away the pain of what happened. I would give anything to rip these pages out of my story and burn them in a pit of fire, and I will fight for the rest of my life to stop the same words from being written in anyone else's story. But it means that I'm reclaiming my life. I'm taking back my story and choosing to continue writing. And it means that when someone else becomes blocked in their own fairytale, I can hopefully provide tools to help them continue turning their pages. This is my story.

When I was just seven years old, I became a survivor of sexual assault.

Just as with 90 per cent of other sexual assault victims, it was a person known to me. And just like so many other disabled and child victims, my voice was pushed deeper down by an inability to speak up, by not understanding the severity of what had happened to me, by thinking it was my own fault due to my inability to recognise social cues and understand situations, and by thinking that compliance was necessary because 'behave and do as you're told' is drilled into us when we are young.

Eighty per cent of intellectually disabled women have been sexually abused. Disabled people are seven times more likely to be a victim of sexual assault than able-bodied people, and autistic girls are at a particularly, scarily high-risk level.

Just like many other children who are victims of sexual assault, I lost my voice and my bubbly, bright, giggly personality as I became overwhelmed with the weight of what had happened to me. I became distant, angry, violently ill and depressed. I was vomiting every night, refused to sleep, spent every day either in tears, screaming or saying nothing at all. I was a shell.

Mum and Dad noticed almost immediately that I'd begun acting differently, and after more than a month of repetitive, adamant questioning and reminders from Mum that I could tell her anything, one night, while she was kissing me goodnight, I tugged on her arm and quietly spilled out my seven-year-old heart to her, recounting everything that had been burning inside of me and eating me alive.

The following morning, police officers came to our home. What followed was a visit to the police station where I had to testify in a room by myself, a sexual assault forensic medical examination that I cried through the whole time, followed by months of attending Child and Adult Mental Health Services (CAMHS), and years more of attending weekly psychology appointments. Even now, this experience affects me daily. I was constantly terrified of any man who wasn't an immediate family member. Today, the number of men I feel safe around is still very small. I can count on one hand the number of nights that I've slept through, nightmare free.

I broke down on multiple occasions throughout my childhood and teenage years because I was positive I would soon need to partake in things that I didn't want to—the idea of marriage or relationships scared me to death. I'm still petrified of intimacy.

I can no longer watch some of my most favourite Disney films because of the memories they bring back. Unexpected movement still causes my body to jump and seize and my skin to prick with fear. And being in a room with people I don't know makes my heart race and my stomach tighten. Every time I see a new film, start a new television series or read a new book, I have to check and double-check any content warnings as even simulated or suggested scenes can send me into a backwards spiral that could take months or years for me to come back from.

I still have weekly meetings with a therapist to help me work through that chapter of my life. It's a chapter that is a part of my story now, written as deeply into the pages as any other part of my story, and with words that spiral into every other aspect of my life.

My PTSD diagnosis that came with this experience is likely one of the main reasons why my autism took a further six years to diagnose. Autism, ADHD and other neurodevelopmental disabilities have multiple overlaps and similarities with PTSD, including a loss of executive functioning, emotional dysregulation, sleep difficulties, lack of interest in peers, social difficulties, poor working memory, repetitive play, increased anxiety, excessive stimming and sensory issues.

Given that I was showcasing typical signs of PTSD, that a known event was the obvious cause, and that the world did not yet recognise the signs of autism in young girls, how could any of the adults in my life have seen anything other than a young child devastated by circumstances?

AUTISM AND ADHD SYMPTOMS THAT OVERLAP PTSD

- ★ inattention
- ★ sleeping problems
- ★ stimming
- ★ impulsivity
- ★ difficulty concentrating
- ★ poor impulse control
- ★ loss of interest
- ★ disorganisation
- ★ poor working memory
- ★ hypervigilence
- ★ emotional numbness
- ★ rejection sensitivity
- ★ easily distracted
- ★ sensory issues
- ★ low self-esteem
- ★ anxiety.

One bad chapter led to another

Eating disorders

As I began to get older, more and more kids started finding their paths while I still felt stuck, lost, like the chopped-down vines of their cleared paths were entangling me, leaving me without the ability to move forward and find my own identity, my own Happily

Ever After. After many, many, many failed attempts to be 'normal', I began to realise that I could never fit in. No matter how hard I tried, no matter how hard I masked who I was, my brain, my outlook, my entire being could never be what was expected or wanted. No matter what, I remained weird. I remained an outcast. I remained cast away, drowning in the screams of what society wanted me to become.

Within the first couple of weeks of high school, I had already received several comments regarding my appearance and weight. My body wasn't the right shape. My boobs were too small. My skin was too pale. My hair was too stringy. My tummy stuck out too much. My eyes were too far apart. My forehead was too big. If there was a part of my body that could be ridiculed, it was. Hell, there were parts of my body that were ridiculed that I wasn't even aware *could* be. Who knew that teeth could be the wrong shape, or that freckles could be in the wrong place? I concluded that I needed to change every bit of my appearance, hoping it would be enough to mask further who I was on the inside so I could finally find my place in this world.

I would love to end this part of my story here. I would so love to say that trying to change my body never made me any more popular or more liked, that I discovered in a matter of days that who I was inside was all that mattered, *yadda yadda yadda*. But unfortunately, that wasn't what happened.

I stopped eating.

It started in small amounts, skipping meals, then I stopped eating altogether. For months, the only food I allowed to pass my lips was what I had deemed 'safe'—meaning, food with no calories and no nutritional value. I started exercising excessively and hid my body beneath oversized band-branded T-shirts and hoodies, so my parents wouldn't notice what was happening. Any time Mum brought it up, I pushed her away dismissively, telling her she was being overly dramatic and that I was fine. My immense love for Nutella was what I used as a cover-up: *See, how can there be anything wrong when I'm eating a tablespoonful of Nutella?*

My body changed dramatically, and so did my health. I couldn't stand for long periods of time without growing dizzy. I forgot the most basic of things. I was constantly exhausted and sick.

I remember the first time one of the popular girls told me I was 'starting to look really pretty'. I had gone for far too long without proper food and had collapsed that morning from an excessive amount of exercise, yet I was absolutely stoked by what she said. It all felt worth it because of that one comment.

I became more socially acceptable because I looked the way they wanted me to. My differences were hidden. I learned that it didn't matter if you're an absolute oddball as long as you have the right, aesthetically pleasing body type.

Nobody cared that my eyes were dead and sunken. Nobody cared that I lost the ability to ride my horses or go surfing with my family. Nobody cared that my hair was falling out, that my skin was yellow and dull, that I was struggling to pay attention in class and made excuses to skip sport because my heart wasn't strong enough for it. No one cared that my teeth and nails were weak and yellow. Nobody cared because I was skinny. I was thin. I took up minimal space in the world.

Our society so deeply values thinness. The cover of every magazine, the model on every poster, the face of every television advertisement shows us what is desirable in a female: tall (but not gangly), skinny (but still with boobs and a bum), tan (but not too tan) and toned (but not muscular)—despite the fact that the women in these photos don't even look like that. At a fashion catwalk I did when I was sixteen that marketed itself to be inclusive, my own body was photoshopped in the photos to appear at least two sizes slimmer than I already was. At 5 foot and 7 inches (170 centimetres) I had the measurements of a child and was five years deep into an eating disorder. And even that wasn't good enough. My dying body wasn't exempt from an impossible ideal.

Alongside these unattainable standards are constant messages about what to be (or not be).

> 'Here's how [insert famous celebrity's name] lost her pregnancy weight in two weeks!'
>
> 'Fight flab! Look fab!'
>
> 'How to stop your hunger cravings.'
>
> '50 worst beach bodies.'
>
> 'The most shocking bikini bodies you've ever seen!'
>
> 'Celebrities who have lost their fight with cellulite.'

And thanks to social media, it's now close to impossible to remove ourselves from this constant beauty ideal. Instagram influencers with their photoshopped waists, false *What I Eat in a Day* videos and paid promotions for waist trainers, weight-loss gummies and skinny teas are presented to us while we simply scroll through our feeds. They're impossible to miss. And because many of these influencers advertise themselves as 'relatable', and 'like us', it's easy to believe that what they're promoting is achievable.

The media has deeply established what it means to be 'beautiful', and that we must meet these standards to be valued. It's no wonder children as young as three are experiencing poor body image. It's no wonder that 81 per cent of ten year olds are afraid of being fat, that by early high school, 70 per cent of girls are unhappy with more than one part of their body, or that 46 per cent of children between the ages of nine and eleven have been on diets, and 50 per cent of teenage girls have used unhealthy and dangerous ways to lose weight. It's no wonder we praise thin bodies, no matter the cost.

But, how goddamn disappointing that when I was at my lowest, I was praised. How depressing. I was so desperate to fit in, to feel some sort of normal, I developed anorexia and bulimia by the age of only twelve.

Anorexia disproportionately affects autistic people, with at least 25 per cent of sufferers being autistic, though many studies suggest it could be as high as 52.5 per cent. Anorexia within autistic people has also been seen time and time again to be much more severe and long lasting than for neurotypical people. Similarly, girls with ADHD are four times more likely to suffer from an eating disorder, and more than half of bulimia sufferers are thought to have ADHD due to our body's inability to feel 'full' while eating, and lack of awareness of hunger in the first place, often leading to binge eating and overeating.

AUTISM AND EATING DISORDERS

While there's no specific reason why anorexia, the most fatal mental health disorder in the world (up to 10 per cent of sufferers die within the first ten years and 20 per cent after twenty years; only 30 per cent fully recover), affects autistic people at such a significantly higher rate than non-autistic people, here are a few things we can consider.

Eating restrictive diets

Seventy per cent of autistic children have issues with food and eating, due to sensory sensitivities and a hypersensitivity to taste and texture. An intense aversion to new foods and foods of different textures or flavours causes many autistic people's diets to be rigid and unchanging.

Thinking that is black-and-white

Black-and-white thinking is often a key part of being autistic, that 'all good or all bad', 'all in or all out' approach often going towards food and diet as well. An inability to find a middle ground can mean that food, clothing sizes and calorie intakes can be seen as either a 'good' thing or a 'bad' thing.

Fitting in

With a world that values both thinness and normality, and our inability to be the latter, succumbing to diet culture to create a seemingly perfect body may be a last resort to fit in and avoid a small amount of the constant, daily ridicule.

Having autism and eating disorder comorbidities

People with social difficulties and who struggle to relate to peers have been proven to be more likely to develop disordered eating habits.

Desiring to take back control

In a world that often feels foreign and out of our control, sometimes the only way we have agency over our situation is by controlling what we can, which might only be our food intake and the size of our bodies.

Regressing

As we get older and reach adulthood, the world may seem increasingly confusing and unaccommodating to disability and neurodivergence. Disordered eating behaviours may be an attempt to regain a sense of safety. *If I'm frail, if I look like a child, I won't have to deal with an adult world that doesn't cater to me.*

Having obsessive tendencies

Our black-and-white thinking and obsessive tendencies can cause 'small' changes to take over our entire beings. It's not just losing a tiny bit of weight, exercising a tiny bit, gaining some sort of control. Instead, these 'little bits' can become anxiety-inducing triggers that can only be reduced by ritualistic compulsions around food, dieting and exercising.

Originally, I believed my eating disorder stemmed from wanting to look like everyone else, a desperation to fit in and hide the so-called 'bad' parts of me with parts that were aesthetically pleasing and valued—and I still believe this, without a doubt. Unquestionably, the straw that broke the metaphorical camel's back was believing that if I could change my body, I could change the way the world saw me. But it was so much deeper than that. Nasty schoolgirl comments and societal expectations aside, my mind had been in a downward spiral for many years. Developing an eating disorder was almost a guarantee.

Spiralling down with no way up

⚠ Mental disorders

Growing up in a world that wasn't created for even the most basic level of my existence meant that I grew up incredibly ostracised and ridiculed. I was taught from a young age that my mind wasn't valued, that my existence wasn't important, that I wasn't supposed to be here. How can a little girl ever find herself when every part of society is telling her that she can't be the only version of herself she has ever known?

The mask that I put on for school every single day to cover up who I truly was and to act out a watered down, allowable version of myself began cracking. If I was lucky, I could keep it on until I returned home to the safety of my family. But most days, the mask would fall off several times and I had to scramble to pick it up and strap it back on. My school life moved between hiding in the back of the library in the fantasy section (where no one ever went) and locking myself in the toilets, as it was the only place in the entire school where I could cry without people hearing me. On one occasion, the tears came too quickly for me to leave the classroom, so I made up an extravagant lie that I was 'crying on command', a pathetic excuse of a joke that I doubt was believed by anyone.

I was exhausted. The light in my body was fading and I had no desire to even be here anymore. What was the point when life was a constant circle of forcing a broken mask onto yourself to survive, only to rip it off at the end of the day to reveal a girl who was just as broken? I had no energy left to be the me I once was—and should still have been. Simply living was a chore.

Asking for help seemed like an impossibility. The rest of the world was able to handle these expectations, so why couldn't I? Asking for help or telling my already worried parents that I wasn't coping felt like a cop out, like admitting defeat. I didn't know it at the time, but I was severely depressed and battling extreme anxiety.

Even after my autism diagnosis, the world felt like a huge, terrifying, uncertain place. I had panic attacks to the point of being hospitalised. Crowds, loud noises and confusing situations caused immediate panic; often I'd wake up afterwards on the floor, my parents by my side as they calmly told me, 'Sweetheart, you just fainted again'. My mental health was forever teetering on a rickety wooden bridge, waiting for the smallest gust of wind to pull it into the rapids below. Or perhaps it was more like a bridge that had already been broken but was on such a secluded path that no one noticed before it was too late.

When I was eighteen, I had a horse-riding accident that caused internal bleeding in two organs, internal bruising, a ruptured bladder, tissue damage, a deep gash and second-degree friction burns, along with the possibility that I would never walk or ride my horses again (the second of which caused me the most distress).

It was a freak accident in a training ring, when a horse went rogue and started running wild. When I saw him coming at full speed towards my pony, I put myself in front of her to protect her—resulting in an 800-kilogram force being pushed into my body. (I've been asked multiple times why I did such a stupid thing, to which I always respond, 'If he had kicked her with that much force, they would have put her down. If he kicked me, they had to try and fix me.' I hold my ground on that argument.) But it was what happened after the accident that made things start to spiral.

Despite the pain, despite passing out, despite my skin being as white as paper and that I was coughing up blood, I was *adamant* against calling an ambulance. Ambulances, doctors, hospitals—anything involving medical treatment—have always been one of my biggest fears. I panic going to get a simple check-up. I feel bile rise to my throat when I see an ambulance whizz past.

When I was a little girl, my nan hurt her hip and they called an ambulance to pick her up. As they were putting her in, the paramedic turned on the siren as a 'fun treat' for me, but I immediately started bawling, having convinced myself that sirens automatically meant death (even though my nan was laughing and chatting away).

So, when the ambulance was inevitably called for me, my mind and body went into panic mode. I panicked when my parents arrived at the scene and I saw Mum in tears. (Still now, in my twenties, I'm convinced that seeing my parents cry means the world is ending.) I panicked when Mum worriedly spoke with the paramedics in a hushed voice. I panicked when they got out scissors to cut off my favourite jeans (my pleas of desperation convinced them to shimmy them off instead). I panicked when a brace was put around my neck, straps were wrapped around my entire body and legs, and I was lifted onto a stretcher without the ability to move. I panicked when I was rushed into the emergency ward and immediately hooked up to what felt like a million different drips, cords, tubes and monitors.

I was strapped to machines, unable to move any part of my body. I was surrounded by people I didn't know, who were touching and poking and prodding me while loud noises surrounded me from every direction. There were MRI machines and a blue dye that made my blood feel hot, and X-rays, and blood tests and catheters and drips and doctors talking in code.

I was living a nightmare.

I'd had horse-riding accidents before—enough that some of the doctors knew me by name. They would laugh when they saw me in the waiting room and say that I clearly hadn't taken up their suggestion to catch butterflies instead of riding horses. But nothing like this had ever happened, nothing this intense, this terrifying.

I was more scared, overwhelmed and overstimulated than I had ever been in my life and there was no escape. My ability to vocalise disappeared, causing me to regress to a mental state that I had not been in for an incredibly long time. My body shut down. I was unable to communicate or make sense of what was happening.

When Mum answered questions that I wasn't capable of answering, I was scolded and told off by the nurses. I was laughed at for being eighteen years old and unable to respond for myself. They eye-rolled and tut-tutted, saying that I needed to have some maturity: 'You are an adult now, you need to act like one.'

And then it hit me.

Having only just turned eighteen, this was my first time in the adult ward, my first time being treated as an adult. No longer were tears and fear and uncertainty seen as just a child who was scared; now they were a pathetic excuse for an adult. No longer were my sensory issues seen as those of a little girl with extra support needs; now I was an adult who was noncompliant and a burden. The nurses became angry when I went non-verbal, and Dad was kicked out of the room simply because he was my dad. My parents were no longer allowed to stay with me.

⚠ Eating disorders

It was my first experience of adulthood and I realised how desperately I did not want to be a part of that world. I formed a deep belief that if I was small, if I was fragile, vulnerable and weak—like a child—I would still have to be looked after. This knowledge of how horrendously society treated disabled adults caused me to continue to regress and initiated the most lethal stage of my eating disorder.

For years after the accident, I battled daily, hourly, minute-by-minute with anorexia. It ruined not just my life, but those of the people surrounding me, too.

I yelled at Mum and poured a smoothie she had made me down the drain because I saw in the rubbish bin a peel from an avocado she had put in it so I would have some form of nutrition that day. I screamed at my auntie and violently sobbed on Christmas day when I found out she had used some of my fear foods in the gingerbread cookies she had made especially for me—knowing that gingerbread has always been my favourite. I sat in silence as Dad held me, watching him cry for the first time in my life as he told me that he was terrified he wouldn't have a little girl anymore if I kept this up.

I had to quit horse competitions and was kicked out of musicals that I had been rehearsing months for, because my parents wouldn't allow me to attend without eating. I deemed not eating more important than participating in the things I adored to do and that were once my entire life source. My eating disorder became all-encompassing; it was the key part of who I was.

When I was twenty-one, after going a few days without solid food and being at the lowest weight I had been in years, Mum grabbed my arm and told me with tears in her eyes that she had found a clinic and I was going to be admitted that week, whether or not I agreed. I became terrified, with flashbacks of the hospital stay entering my mind. I begged her to give me another chance, begged her to allow me to just try. With both of us crying, Mum gave a quiet 'okay'.

I'm now further into recovery than I have ever been, and I continue to progress every single day. I don't believe I will ever 'fully recover', despite those around me telling me that I look better, that I seem better. Daily, I have to push back nagging thoughts, tell them to back off, to not let them take over again. Daily, I have to choose recovery. But it's a battle that I'm finally winning.

I can now eat three meals a day, plus snacks, and not hear my head shouting at me that I ate too much. I can now have cake at parties, enjoy takeaway night with my family, and eat treats at the movies without telling myself I'll have to 'make up for it' tomorrow, or simply decline the offer altogether. Hell, I can eat treats whenever I want.

Putting a moral compass and claiming some food as 'good' and some food as 'bad' is absolute hogwash, anyway. The only food that is bad is food that does not serve you mentally, emotionally and physically. Before I did my first *Vogue* shoot, I had burgers and hot chips the previous night. I actively chose to eat my favourite dessert the night before filming more revealing scenes for *Heartbreak High*. I refuse to believe that my body is less valuable because I eat, that it is less desirable because there may be more of it.

I have succumbed to diet culture for too long, I have lost too many years of my life to worrying about my body. And, while I know there will inevitably be a million more battles, a million more times that I have to actively remind myself to choose recovery (hell, it's a daily chore when you're in an industry that is built off the diet culture with impossible standards in the first place), it's a battle that I'm equipped for. Anorexia nervosa can suck my big toe. My body is no longer available for the diet industry to profit off. I've got better things to do than fit into unrealistic standards of beauty so the already rich can make more money from my self-doubt.

⚠ Chronic illness

At the age of twenty-three, I was diagnosed with postural orthostatic tachycardia syndrome (POTS), a chronic illness and disorder of the autonomic nervous system. This is the part of our body that controls essential bodily functions, such as heart rate, breathing, blood pressure, sleep cycles and temperature control. (If it happens naturally, our autonomic nervous system is the one to thank for it.) This condition means that while a healthy person's nervous system will ensure a sufficient amount of blood reaches the brain, mine plainly and simply cannot be bothered.

The effect of this *'No thanks, you're on your own, babes, lmao xo'* attitude of said nervous system is that my body has constant tachycardia (abnormally high heart rate), chronic fatigue, low blood pressure, migraines, heart palpitations, brain fog and memory issues, fainting and dizzy spells, nausea, blurred vision and struggles with physical activity. My body uses about three times more energy than that of a healthy person because my heart beats the same number of times in one day that a healthy person's does in three. A task like standing is the equivalent to constantly running on the spot.

While the cause of POTS can vary, many people develop it after a viral illness or traumatic event, and it's believed that one in ten POTS patients has ADHD. In my case, we believe the cause was ten years of eating disorders on top of PTSD.

Despite having had symptoms of POTS since childhood, having gone to various clinics and undergone many heart monitoring tests and numerous medical assessments, I fell in that 85 per cent of POTS patients who are incorrectly diagnosed with poor mental health and told 'It's all in your head' prior to receiving a diagnosis. Twenty-five per cent of POTS patients become so ill that they can no longer work or attend school, and in some cases, patients end up in a wheelchair or bedbound. And still, despite these statistics, I was like so many others harmed by the health system. I merely accepted that 'it's all in your head' attitude to the point where, for years, I was using it as an example of my anxiety when I would publicly share my story: 'My anxiety was so bad that I thought I had a heart condition!'

You did, girl. And you were gaslighted by the medical industry.

There are so many correlations between neurodivergence, poor mental health and chronic illness. These are incredibly misunderstood by society, and it is so deeply important that we educate ourselves about and destigmatise them, both within the wider community and within ourselves.

Mental illness and neurodiversity

⚠ Suicide, mental health and eating disorders

While each person's mental health journey is as unique as the larger fairytale that holds it, the types of struggles I've experienced are all too common for neurodivergent and disabled people. Growing up in a world that belittles, condemns and stigmatises differences is a recipe for poor mental health. Our world has never once shown us that we as disabled people belong here, unless we can drastically change every part of ourselves to fit with societal norms and expectations, which for many of us is simply not an option.

Society is so belittling of disabled people that studies have shown that suicide is perceived as significantly more acceptable for the disabled, and that health services are lacking and inaccessible for those who need them most. When it comes to mental health and disabled folk, no one is ready to discuss it. Why are there are so many comorbidities? Why are there accessibility issues for mental health support services? These discussions are not even put on the table.

At the moment, mental health barriers are a huge concern in the autistic community. *This is why* in the United Kingdom suicide is the leading cause of early death in autistic people. *This is why* autistic people are more than nine times more likely to die by suicide and twenty-eight times more likely to consider it. *This is why* 70 per cent of autistic people have mental health conditions. *This is why* an autistic person's lifespan is on average 26 years shorter than that of a non-autistic person—if we make it to our fifty-fourth birthday, we've beaten the odds.

In Australia, 49 per cent of autistic adults have had immense difficulty finding and accessing clinical mental health support and have expressed worry and low confidence in the health system and health professionals' understanding of autism. More than 90 per cent of autistic adults have challenges accessing health care, with 33 per cent completely unable to access mental health support.

There are multiple reasons why we have barriers receiving the correct mental health care, including low awareness and understanding of autism within the medical field, communication difficulties (especially when a person may be non- or selectively verbal), sensory sensitivities (often heightened in stressful environments) and a lack of collaboration between mental health, physical health and disability services as well as the education, employment, justice and housing sectors.

Autistic eating disorder patients have far less effective treatment outcomes than their non-autistic peers, partly due to the fact that treatment of any sort, in either physical or mental health, rarely accommodates autistic people's needs and doesn't focus on the reason behind the disorder in the first place.

And while autistic and otherwise disabled people are disproportionately at risk, it's not like the rest of our mental health sector is sunshine and rainbows. Suicide is the leading cause of death for Australians between the ages of fifteen and forty-four, and 54 per cent of people experiencing poor mental health will not speak up or ask for help. More than 10 per cent of those with a chronic mental health condition will die by suicide within the first ten years of their diagnosis, and having a chronic health condition increases the odds of attempting suicide by 363 per cent.

Suicide rates of Indigenous Australians are almost double those of the non-indigenous community, with 5.2 per cent of deaths being from suicide. LGBTQIA+ folk are more than five times as likely to die by suicide than cisgender or heterosexual individuals. Yet we live in a society that constantly preaches kindness on the internet, that has R U OK? days, #SuicidePreventionDay and #WorldMentalHealthDay, and that promises to end bullying in schools and workplaces. We decorate our social-media feeds with trending hashtags and see ourselves as progressive and forward thinking. We preach that we need to end the stigma until we're blue in the face, that we need to open up to our loved ones and reach out when we're struggling—but it's all performative.

It's fake. It's false. Because when someone is struggling, no one bats an eyelid. Because when I spent every year of my life struggling with depression, anxiety, PTSD and eating disorders, no one thought to look towards me. Because we turn a blind eye to poor mental health, when I was dealing with a life-altering chronic health condition that had my body attacking itself, I was told by the medical field to 'just breathe'.

We live in a society that stigmatises mental health, in which just the term 'mental health' is taboo and unspoken, and yet it's something each and every one of us has. If you don't see a doctor when you're suffering from poor physical health you're seen as crazy, while if you *do* see a doctor for poor mental health you're seen as, well, crazy. Mental health shouldn't be associated with negativity, horror movies, sickness and despair. It shouldn't be associated with weakness, fragility or feebleness. It should be associated with all of us, with our everyday, with our *always*.

Taking charge of your mental health is okay.

Talking about your mental health is okay.

Talking about your ill mental health is okay.

It is okay to reach out, to seek help, to need someone. Because the bottom line is that we all need help sometimes. Everything needs help to grow. Even the most beautiful flower in the most beautiful garden withers away without care, even the waves would vanish without the moon to guide them, even the moon needs the sun's light to shine in the night sky. Who are you to believe that you don't need the same support?

SIGNS SOMEONE MAY BE STRUGGLING WITH POOR MENTAL HEALTH

The emphasis is on 'may be' here. It's not always easy to tell when someone is struggling or needing help, but these signs may be an indicator that they are.

Changes in behaviour

- ★ no longer participating in activities they once enjoyed
- ★ isolating themselves from friends and family
- ★ sleeping more but still feeling tired
- ★ being less productive at school and work
- ★ loss or gain in appetite
- ★ increased alcohol and drug use
- ★ impaired judgement.

Changes in appearance

- ★ neglecting basic hygiene and care, such as not brushing teeth and hair and wearing dirty clothing
- ★ frequently looking tired, dull, sad or 'numb'
- ★ dramatic, fast weight loss or gain.

Changes in mood

- ★ feeling sad or hopeless all the time
- ★ trouble coping with everyday life
- ★ heightened stress or anxiety levels
- ★ lashing out
- ★ over- or under-reacting to situations.

Changes in speech

- ★ speaking negatively about themselves
- ★ expressing physical complaints such as 'I don't feel well'
- ★ disinterest in life (that is, 'What's the point?').

Changes in what they post online

- ★ posting dark poetry, songs or photos
- ★ using sad, distressed emoticons
- ★ posting negative comments
- ★ using negative hashtags.

SIGNS OF POOR MENTAL HEALTH IN A NEURODIVERGENT PERSON

In neurodivergent people, the signs of poor mental health listed above still remain, but there may be other key features to look out for.

They are in constant burnout

Burnout is a sign that someone is overwhelmed and struggling, while frequent burnout may indicate a deeper struggle and need for help. See page 69 for signs of burnout.

More frequent repetitive and compulsive behaviour

Autistic folk often have repetitive and compulsive behaviours, but if these begin to showcase more frequently than usual, or the behaviours have more impact on their mental health, this may be a sign that they are struggling.

Emotional outbursts

Seemingly random, impulsive bursts of negative emotion, often shown as anger, sadness or crying.

Negative stimming

When self-soothing methods turn into self-destructive behaviours, such as head banging, hitting, biting, and so on.

Obsessing over death and depressive art

This includes dark poetry and films, and suicide talk.

WHAT TO DO IF YOU SEE SIGNS OF POOR MENTAL HEALTH IN SOMEONE ELSE

The signs of poor mental health will show up differently in individuals. Sometimes these signs seem obvious but there is no simple way of knowing. If someone is struggling with mental health, there are a number of ways you can support them.

Find a time to gently open the conversation with no distractions

Ensure the space is private and without distractions such as other people, mobile phones, other plans, and so on.

Validate their feelings

Do not be dismissive of what they're feeling with statements such as, 'Cheer up', 'Snap out of it' or 'I'm sure it will pass'.

Do not blame them or put their struggles on you or others with statements such as, 'This is really hard on me, too', or 'You're hurting everyone with the way you're acting' or 'Others have it worse than you'.

Do not say 'I know how you feel' if you don't—this can be incredibly dismissive and invalidating.

Do not use stigmatising words such as 'psycho' or 'crazy'.

Keep questions open-ended—ask, 'Why don't you tell me how you're feeling?' rather than 'I think you may be depressed'.

Offer support

Don't offer more than you're capable of. If you are not a registered counsellor, doctor or psychologist, you are not expected to offer mental health advice—but that doesn't mean you can't help. Offer to go on walks with them, to go out for a coffee, to cook meals and help clean for them.

Offer and remind them of services such as their GP or a specific mental health support service. See pages 257–64 for a list of services.

Listen

The best thing you can do is listen without judgement.

Look after yourself

Poor mental health takes a toll on everyone and it's vital to look after yourself when caring for someone going through a period of poor mental illness. Educate and inform yourself with quality, evidence-based information and become familiar with signs and symptoms of poor mental health, both within yourself and other people. Reach out for help when you need it.

Caring for your mental health

Caring for my mental health is still something I have to make a conscious effort to do daily. I see a psychologist weekly, I need reminders to take breaks, and I take steps to make sure I'm not burning myself out. But 'down days' are inevitable. We're human, we live in a crazy world. Bad days, yuck times and moments that feel less than a fairytale are only to be expected. But we don't have to let them define us. We don't have to let them swallow us whole.

Happy endings are coming, but they take time. Yours is just around the river bend. Here are a few things that can help to keep you on the track to your Happy Ever After.

DOWN DAY CHECKLIST

Make yourself comfortable

First and foremost, the most important thing for a sensory overload day is a 'sensory-no-thanks' outfit. Put on your favourite trackie daks and your favourite band tee from that One Direction concert in 2012, when your life absolutely peaked. Or put on your matching grandma PJs and favourite fuzzy socks—whatever makes you feel comfortable and safe.

Fashion isn't the goal here. We're not here to be an Insta-baddie (unless, of course, that's what *makes* you feel comfortable, in which case go for it). Your job is to feel at your most comfortable, your most cosy, your most 'I'm clocking out for the day'.

Adjust your environment

When you're in sensory overload, your body is telling you that your senses have had too much and can't handle anything that may up the intensity, so you owe it to yourself to ensure that your environment is helping rather than creating further hindrance. As I explained in Chapter 3, this means low, soft, warm lighting—instead of overhead lights, use a salt lamp, a warm-toned desk lamp in the corner of the room or fairy lights. It means using noise-cancelling headphones or decibel-reducing earplugs and playing gentle music.

Listen to yourself, listen to your mind, listen to your body. What do you need? And what do you need to stay away from? You're the expert on yourself, and it's important to surround yourself with things that are going to benefit you.

Rest

Rest is crucial to reset your mind and body. If you continue to overwork and overstimulate yourself, you're going to run the risk of meltdown, burnout or long-term side effects. So, *R. E. S. T.*

No one is expecting you to be a superhero continuously, no one is expecting you to go on and on forever without needing a break to regenerate. Have a bubble bath filled with a million bath bombs and turn the lights off. Make a nest of blankets and pillows and put on your favourite childhood film that you've watched 137 times and can recite line for line. Curl up with a guided meditation and practise your breathing. Do whatever is going to help you.

You are not a product, you are not an item. You are a human being who needs rest, and that is fine.

Create

Nothing big, nothing important, and nothing necessarily good. No one's asking you to write Mozart's 9th Symphony, paint a Picasso or master a craft within the next fifteen minutes. Paint your nails, get out your oil paints and go nuts, journal your feelings, be mindful with a colouring book. Art is therapeutic. Creating things puts our focus on something positive and simple, and can give us time to rest, relax and recover.

Stim

We've spoken about it before, we'll speak about it again, and continue to do so until it's locked in our heads, as accepted and common knowledge as the sky is blue. Stimming. Is. Good. Stim, you beautiful human being. Because it wakes up the nervous system and releases beta-endorphins and happy feel-good chemicals. Stim, because it's vital for you to do so. Stim, because your body needs it, because it is natural. (Go back to page 54 to find a stim that works best for you.)

Go outside

While the idea of staying curled up inside your little cocoon may sound like the most appealing thing in the world, staying inside and in one position all day long isn't a good idea either. When we're in sensory overload, the world can feel too big, too loud, too much, and so our brains try to protect us by forcing our bodies into hibernation mode. However, sensory overload days have the potential to slip into depressive episodes. Learn to listen to your brain and ask it what you need. No one's asking you to climb a mountain or run a marathon or go skydiving, but step outside and walk your dog, practise some simple yoga, simply sit outside and *be*.

Declutter

This may be the last thing you want to do when your brain is feeling yuck, but if your space is also yuck, it's not going to help your situation. Do something simple: refold your T-shirts, organise your books . . . you'll be surprised how much lighter you can feel if your safe space is also a clean space. (God, I sound like my mum.)

Fuel yourself

Finding the energy to eat or drink may be difficult when you're in sensory overload, but it's important that we continue to do so anyway. On my sensory overload days, I tend to settle for pre-made foods, a big bottle of water that I won't have to get up and refill, and lots and lots of tea—a hot tea is like a warm hug involving absolutely no other people and exactly what you need when you're in sensory overload.

Remember to eat, remember to drink. Food is fuel—physical fuel and emotional fuel.

Have a cuddle

I know what you're thinking. *But Chloé, I don't want to be around people when my brain feels like it's imploding and I would quite enjoy the idea of escaping from my skin right now.* I hear you, I feel you, I am you. So instead, wrap yourself up in a weighted blanket or cuddle a pet. These activities release dopamine and serotonin, both of which are neurological transmitters that relieve anxiety, stress and depression and are proven to make you happier and calmer. So, scientifically speaking, giving your pet a cuddle is going to make you feel better.

Happy endings are coming, but they take time. Yours is just around the river bend.

CHAPTER 6

Seeking a Diagnosis

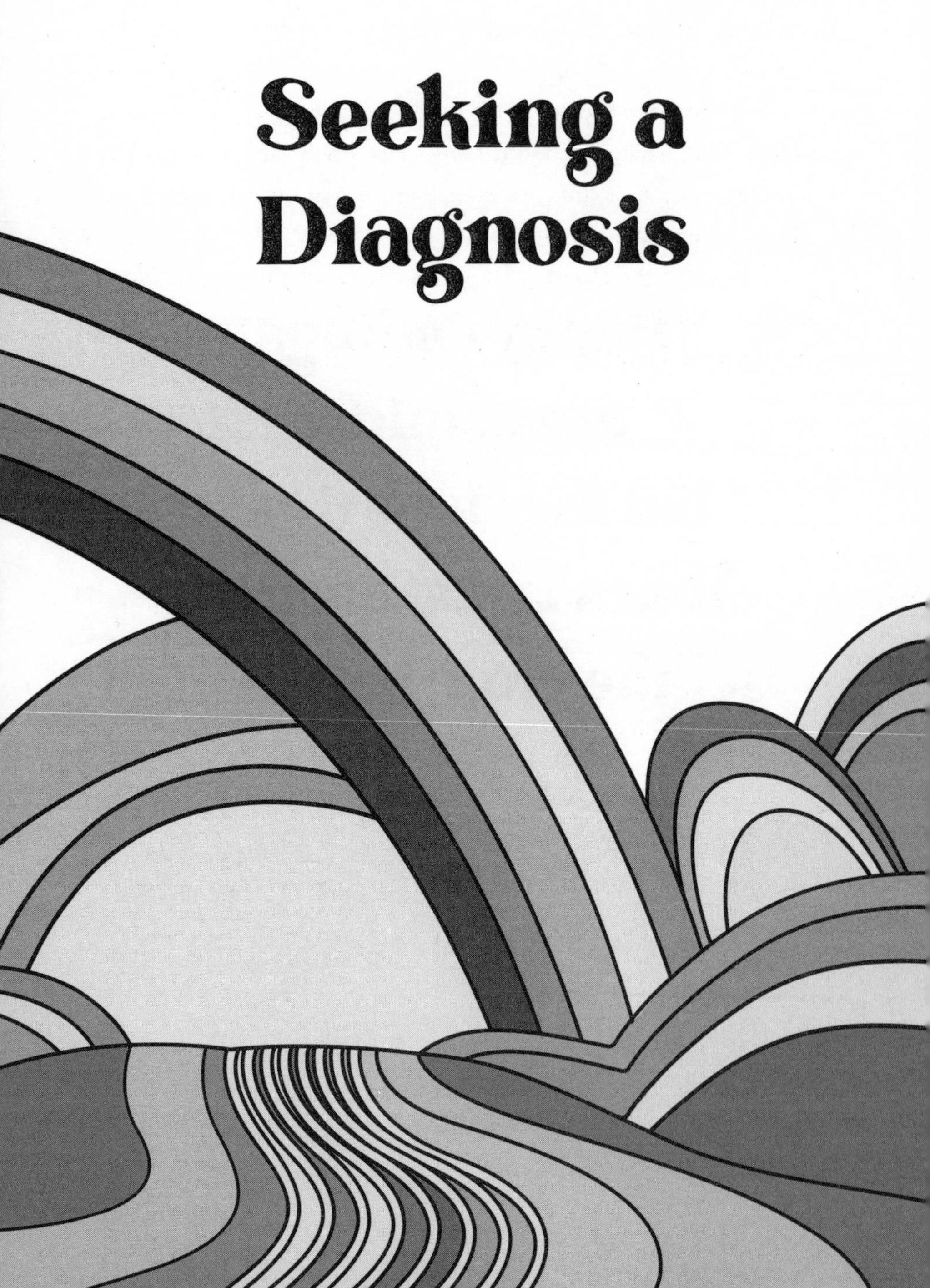

We live in a highly media-based and visual world, where we tend to have a 'seeing is believing' approach. We take print and television at face value without ever choosing to look more closely at the group that it's supposedly representing.

We see advertisements telling us we can never be beautiful unless we're whatever specific body shape is currently in style. We inevitably end up telling ourselves that we're not worthy unless we reach these specific and unrealistic goals.

We see news reports that negatively highlight specific races, religions, communities, disabilities or groups, and it's often ingrained into us to be fearful, to exclude the different-from-us simply because they're different from us. Simply because we have been told to do so.

We see people falsely portraying disability, whether on a television show with a neurotypical actor putting on a horrid performance of autism, or in fearmongering news articles that show disabilities as a specific type of person, with a specific type of disability. We believe this is the only way someone can be disabled, particularly when the disability is used as a drawcard, as a reason, as a blame.

We see neurodiversity from a perspective of what's been incorrectly taught to us, rather than what it really is. We only consider what Hollywood, newspaper articles and stereotyped ideologies have presented. We think of Sheldon Cooper in *The Big Bang Theory*, we think of Raymond in *Rain Man*, we think of Arnie in *What's Eating Gilbert Grape*, we think of a man we saw on the news, we think of our neighbour's best friend's brother's baker whose ex-wife's dog's breeder has a son you suspect is autistic (so therefore you know everything about it).

We will take every perspective in the world on it . . . except listening to an autistic person themself.

When we hear the word 'autism', many of us will often think of the same, stereotypical idea: a cisgender white male with poor social skills and an obsession with trains and science, or a child (once again, male) extensively stimming and screaming down the aisles of a supermarket. We believe it so deeply that even our medical and autism diagnostic system is built entirely off gender and media-based stereotypes that are not even remotely considered genuine diagnostic traits.

So, when a young girl who's displayed classic autism symptoms throughout her entire life goes completely unnoticed by the system that is supposed to support and help her—well, we can't really be surprised, can we?

Not just 'quirky'

I had been showcasing classic autism traits throughout my entire life, but a diagnosis was never something that was put on the table. Reading back through these chapters, it seems unbelievable to me that a diagnosis took so long—I may as well have been wearing a large, glowing neon sign that said 'autistic'. But the delay was likely because of the stereotypes our society has about autism.

> 'She's a girl, so it can't be autism.'
> 'She doesn't act like [insert male autistic character from mainstream media].'
> 'She communicates well.'
> 'She functions like the rest of us.'

So, I was left feeling every bit an alien, with absolutely no understanding of who I was, no explanation for why this planet was so confusing, no answer as to why I knew I was different, despite no

WHAT'S IN A NAME?

Neurodiversity is a term used to describe neurological conditions such as autism, ADHD, dyslexia, dyspraxia and Tourette's syndrome. The term was originally coined in 1998 by Australian sociologist Judy Singer to challenge the idea that certain neurodevelopmental disorders were inherently pathological. Singer put forward a new social model of disability, with the understanding that it is the social barriers facing those of us with different wiring that are the main factors disabling people.

To put it simply, and quite beautifully, the concept of neurodiversity calls on us to recognise and respect neurological differences as you would any other human variation. It is simply the result of normal differences in the human genome, and a showcasing of how wonderfully diverse the human population is. Trying to 'correct' someone's neurodiversity—as people once tried (and unfortunately, still try) to do—is taking away that person and all that they are.

We need to reject the idea that autism, ADHD and any other form of neurodiversity can and should be cured, advocating instead to celebrate the difference in neurodiversity and all forms of communication and self-expression.

Neurodiversity supports the idea that we need to create systems that support our minds, and to allow neurodivergent people to live as they are.

one else being able to tell, except for the occasional, 'She's very . . . odd, isn't she? (But don't worry, she'll grow out of it.)'

My parents, being fairly young and the only ones with a child in their immediate circle, had no other children for comparison when I started displaying classic autism symptoms, so for the most part they considered me fairly normal.

As a baby, I cried almost constantly, and I screamed bloody murder unless Dad wrapped me so tightly in a swaddle that freeing myself from an escape jacket would have proven easier. I refused to sleep unless it was on Dad's chest and with deep pressure on my back in the form of one of my parents having to pat my back for hours, or their ingenious invention of lying a teddy over the top of me to simulate that same pressure and heaviness.

As I grew, the pretty little dresses and matching headbands that Mum so desperately wanted to dress her firstborn in were left hanging in the wardrobe, as I became a screaming banshee at even a breath of the fabric touching me. Much to my incredibly fashionable Mum's dismay, I would only wear those horrendous matching tracksuit sets that I preferred for days on end.

Autism can become much more apparent in childhood and adolescence, particularly in girls when social barriers are often more visible. While this was evidently the case for me, the child psychologists merely said, 'It's PTSD, and it's expected after what she's been through.' And so, it was left at that.

Chloé: Weird, quirky, different. A little bit broken, but life goes on.

By the age of thirteen, midway through Year 8, the feeling of living on an alien planet was more obvious and debilitating than ever. My mental health had been steadily declining, my school attendance was dismal, and my performance on the rare occasion that I was at school was crumbling and a clear outward expression of my poor mental health. I was struggling. My dragons were becoming far too strong, the elephant graveyard was becoming far too dark, the chapters of my fairytale were being ripped apart, and the author in me was unable to continue writing.

Finally, my English teacher was the first one to take action, calling my parents in for an emergency after-school meeting. It was a meeting I was not invited to—Mum told me years later it involved displays of my recent schoolwork, a showcase of my exceedingly disorganised locker, and the lost property box, in which 95 per cent of items belonged to me. It was also an explanation that I wasn't up to the expectations in either the work ethic, work standard, or mental capacity of the other students. It finished with a cautious suggestion of getting some tests done because 'there may be something wrong with her'.

How disappointing that we live in a society where a child is either completely 'normal'—as in, they can fit into this oddly designed box that no one in particular created but that society has deemed to be the only way—or there's something entirely, utterly, absolutely wrong with them.

'Wrong' was first tested by a visit to the hospital to get a CT scan for brain damage. 'They think you hurt yourself from falling off Marlea too many times,' Mum explained when I asked her why they needed to test my brain. Apparently, those falls off my little crossbred pony—my best friend in the entire world—was the first reason they considered for my actions, mind and apparent wrongness.

I had fallen off Marlea more times than I could count over the three months since I'd owned her, and she had sent me to hospital for concussions at least once a month within that time. Now, I was no longer allowed to ride unless Dad was leading her, even though I had been riding since I was four. She'd also been banned from the local pony club after biting a dressage instructor on the boob. But, she was *my* psychotic little pony, and I loved her on a level that I had never loved anything.

My heart sank.

If she was the reason for why I was too different, was she really going to be taken from me? And what was so wrong with me? Was I really so awful that brain damage and horse-riding accidents were being considered the cause of my apparent differences?

I was incredibly confused, and felt my heart break, partly because Dad's previous threats to send my beloved demon pony to the knackery had a high potential of coming true if they did find anything. And now because I was aware that my parents' meeting with my teacher the night before must have had something to do with my abilities.

The brain scan results showed absolutely nothing remarkable, which I assumed to be a relief, but apparently it only meant that other avenues needed to be explored. Within the week, I found myself sitting in yet another doctor's office, my attention moving between a massive stack of old *National Geographic* magazines and a large, illustrated poster of whales hanging in the receptionist's office. (It was a ridiculous drawing because the two species in it couldn't possibly swim together; belugas prefer cold arctic waters, while bryde whales prefer tropical waters—one of them would have been horribly uncomfortable.) I didn't understand why I was sitting in this office, but I didn't overly care—I was far too busy reading *National Geographic: Inside Egypt's Secret Vaults* and questioning the whale painter's artistic choices.

When I was called in, a woman with curly hair and glasses perched on her nose greeted me and introduced herself as Janine. Over several hours, I answered her questions, watched her jot down notes that seemed entirely irrelevant, acted out scenes and did quizzes. I felt a sense of utter pride when she asked me to name all of the animals I knew in three minutes. As the timer ended, she asked me how I knew 132 different horse breeds, seventy species of whale, and 'What on earth is a Babirusa?' (I also had to make her aware of the errors in the whale painting outside her office.)

Still, I didn't entirely understand *why* I was there, or why the glasses-lady was asking me seemingly pointless questions (though,

I'd come to expect oddness from most other humans . . . you lot are a bizarre bunch). Or why I was kicked out of the room so she could 'just have a little chat with Mum'. (I was convinced she was going to try and test Mum on her animal knowledge, too—ha, good luck trying to name fifty-seven shark species like I did, Mum.)

That 'little chat with mum' resulted in me seeing Dr Janine every week for the following six weeks, each appointment coming with various tests, games, quizzes and questions that still made absolutely no sense to me, and a final 'chat with Mum' at the end of it all.

When Mum walked out of the office after the final chat, she told me to set down *National Geographic: Secrets of the Whales* so we could leave. My initial reaction was 'How can I send this magazine to the whale artist so he can get his facts straight?' My second was, *Oh. Mum's sad.*

We walked out of the office in silence, Mum carrying a stack of paperwork and a large textbook. I know that I'm not great with understanding social cues, but the rigidity and unease that filled the air could have definitely been cut with a knife. I could feel Mum's sadness deep down in my tummy, making it twist and turn.

Mum had promised me hot chips from our favourite local chicken and chip shop, as well as a Cookies N Cream frappé from our favourite coffee shop that we had recently nicknamed 'Gloria Janine's', after the psychologist. I was beginning to grow anxious. Had I done something wrong that would warrant going home without the treats? Maybe my role play with the glasses-lady, where I'd acted out my morning routine, had revealed some sort of awful thing. Maybe I had offended the doctor with my animal knowledge or comments on her inaccurate whale poster. Maybe it was something worse . . .

After we got into the car, Mum turned on the ignition, and then sat in silence for some time. I noticed her eyes growing wet with tears. When you're thirteen and you see your mum crying, you think the whole world is ending. When you're thirteen and you see your mum crying, and you know it's because of you, you think the whole world is ending and you're the one who's single-handedly making it end.

With that same sick feeling in my tummy that I knew all too well, I worked up the courage to ask Mum the question that I was sure was the only obvious answer. With a quiet, shaky voice, I asked her what I thought had to be the sole cause of the recent doctor's visits, the brain scan, the private meeting, and then the tears following on.

'Mum, am I dying?'

I don't know what thoughts went through Mum's head when her daughter fearfully asked that question, but I imagine they were ones of sadness, of surprise, and a quick realisation that she needed to be a parent now, there wasn't time for wallowing in pity. With a shaken laugh she said, 'No, you're not dying', which did little to quell my fears. I glanced at the book in her hands, hoping for some form of clarity. That was when I took notice of words that I hadn't heard of before and realised that it must be the cause of her tears, and my apparent new illness: *Ass Burger.*

The diagnosis would seemingly not kill me but had labelled me as the bum of a burger. *Absolutely bloody great. All in all, a fair and reasonable explanation for the sea of tears, if you ask me.*

Following another confused question from me, and another tearful laugh from Mum, she confirmed that I did not have a burger ass, nor did I have my secondary guess of *Asparagus*.

'You have Asperger's syndrome, baby,' she told me, as she looked into the rear-view mirror to wipe the mascara that had smudged down her cheeks. 'And it's not something new, it's not something scary. It's just the way your brain works. If you have it, you've always had it—it just took us thirteen years to figure it out. That's why I'm sad.'

Asperger's syndrome? Huh?

Still confused, worried and scared, we drove home in almost silence. I wasn't convinced this new diagnosis wasn't a death sentence. But we got those chicken-salt hot chips and a frappé. So, silver linings.

Arriving home, I quickly retreated to my bedroom and opened up my laptop with missing keys and peeling off One Direction stickers to type these new words into the Google search bar. My heart sank as I read the search results.

Asperger's syndrome: How To Cure It
A Life Ruined by Autism
Support Groups in My Area for Parents Crushed by Autism
Autism: The Devastating Diagnosis

I read through page after page of research papers by self-proclaimed professionals and educational adverts—one even showed autism modelled like a horror-movie villain, with the voice-over stating, 'I am autism. I make it impossible for your family to attend any event without embarrassment and pain. I will make sure your marriage fails. I am autism. You ignored me. That was a mistake. If you are not scared, you should be.' I read fearmongering articles claiming that a life with autism was barely a life at all, and it negatively affected everyone surrounding someone with it.

My inner world flipped and my heart sank. Autism wasn't a death sentence . . . it was so much worse.

Now, I wasn't just *Chloé: weird, quirky, different.*

I was *Chloé: weirdly, devastatingly, ruined by autism.*

A model fit for . . . males

In the first *Diagnostic and Statistical Manual of Mental Disorders* (*DSM*), published in 1952, autism was defined as 'childhood schizophrenia' and 'child psychosis'. It was considered to present differently to typical schizophrenic children due to 'immaturity' and 'plasticity', and to be caused by 'cold parenting' and emotionless mothers.

It wasn't until 1980, in the third edition of the *DSM*, that autism gained its own official diagnosis, described as a 'pervasive developmental disorder' that (go figure) had nothing to do with schizophrenia (although it explained that autistic individuals were likely to develop schizophrenia in adulthood). With fifty test subjects now involved, thirty-nine of whom were male, the *DSM-III* now required six points of diagnostic criteria, listing the essential features of autism to be:

1. pervasive lack of responsiveness to other people
2. gross deficits in language
3. peculiar speech patterns, if speech is present at all
4. bizarre responses to various aspects of the environment
5. rigid and peculiar attachment to objects
6. an absence of delusions, hallucinations, loosening of associations and incoherence, as in schizophrenia.

And these symptoms *had to* be evident before thirty months of age.

In 1987, the updated *DSM-III-R* significantly altered the criteria, allowing for somewhat 'mild' autism to exist, dropping the idea that it must be diagnosed before thirty months, and listing sixteen diagnostic criteria, eight of which had to be met for a clinical diagnosis. These criteria included 'a lack of the awareness of the existence of others' feelings' (as an example, it said that an autistic person 'treats other people as if they're a piece of furniture'), 'gross impairment to make friendship' and 'abnormalities in the production of speech'.

While never directly stated, the 1987 revised manual implied that autism existed on a 'spectrum', an ideology that Hans Asperger (a man who will, unfortunately, make a comeback later in this chapter) had been using since 1944 and one of the leading reasons why autism criteria are still so incredibly biased and rooted in a history of ableism, sexism and misunderstanding.

As I write this, it's believed that around 1 in 160 people are autistic, although many studies showcase it to be as high as 1 in 50. Ninety-eight per cent of Australians have heard of autism, and 86 per cent of people are in close contact with an autistic person. (A statistic that is written poorly, as it makes us sound alien, or like a virus . . . although, that is exactly what we're made to feel like. So, go figure.)

Despite autism being the third most-common developmental disability (with intellectual disabilities being the first, followed by cerebral palsy), and almost everyone in the world having heard of autism with a really basic understanding of what it is, why then was a thirteen year old left sobbing in her bedroom because this diagnosis left her with such rigid fear?

Why was Mum left crying because she'd been told that her daughter was diagnosed with it?

Why are autistic people four times more likely to experience depression than other groups?

Why do we so deeply fear something that is a core part of who we are?

While I continued researching, I noticed another thing that only added more fear and confusion to my already terrified mind.

Not a single one of these articles spoke about autism in women, or adults. It was all directly aimed at male children.

Fabulous. Now, I wasn't just *Chloé: weird, quirky, different.*

I was *Chloé: weirdly, devastatingly, ruined by autism . . . AND a complete abnormality.*

Perfect. Stupendous. Just what a thirteen-year-old girl really needs to kick-start her teenage years.

The autism diagnostic system is built entirely around stereotypical male autistic traits that were determined by studying predominantly male subjects and using clinical tools designed to fit the male autism phenotype. Women are therefore often undiagnosed. Currently, boys are four times more likely to be diagnosed than their female counterparts. The numbers and statistics tell us that women are unlikely to be autistic (or even that females *cannot* be autistic, according to some doctors . . . who should have their licences revoked), but this doesn't mean that there are fewer autistic women. It simply shows that gender gaps exist in every aspect of our lives, including medical diagnostic criteria supposedly built to help us but which often causes further confusion and ostracisation.

Women aren't less likely to be autistic than men—in fact, a new study shows that there may actually be more autistic women than men. We need to look at the system that was created to diagnose it in the first place, a system that is built on sexism, classism and racism, and therefore not accommodating many of the people who need it most.

Autism is incredibly underdiagnosed in women as well because we are socialised to hide key parts of our identity to avoid being seen as too bossy, too much, too little, or too [insert misogynistic term that only applies to women]. Women learn to be more reserved, shy and quiet in order to be the picture-perfect face of femininity and to avoid abuse and misogyny. The result is that autism in women is overlooked and unseen or misdiagnosed as anxiety, depression or bipolar disorder. In turn, our system and social ideologies of gender negatively affect men, with personality disorders being wildly underdiagnosed due to men being expected and nurtured to act explosively and narcissistically.

We women have been taught to disguise ourselves all throughout our lives, so it's easy for us to disguise the fact that we're autistic. *Bright lights? Loud noises? Not understanding social cues? Couldn't be me.* We become masters of disguise because we *need* to, and then it backfires on us when medical professionals turn us away because our traits don't line up with what's expected, even when they are classic autism traits.

Diagnosing autism

HOW AUTISM IS 'EXPECTED' TO PRESENT

These are still considered valid diagnostic criteria by experts, though they are often more in line with male diagnostic criteria.

Lack of emotion

Autistic people may find it difficult to recognise emotions, facial expressions and other emotional cues, including tone of voice and body language. Missing these cues can mean they struggle to show their emotions and to understand those of others.

Peculiar speech patterns

Autistic people may speak more loudly than is deemed acceptable. They may also use monotonous and unusually formal tones, both in the enunciation of words and the tone itself, often due to an inability to recognise tone and the pitch within their own voice and speech patterns.

Unimaginative play

Rather than playing with toys conventionally, autistic children may interact with toys in a more repetitive and unimaginative way, including lining them up and/or sorting them by colour and size.

Strict adherence to rules and need for structure

Autistic people rely on predictable, safe, structured environments and routines to feel grounded and safe. Deviations and sudden changes from these structures and routines can result in extreme anxiety and lead to meltdowns.

Lack of empathy

Autistic people are often described as lacking empathy and unable to feel what others are feeling.

Fascination for dates and small details

A 'fascination' with dates, numbers, patterns and small details has long been considered typical in an autism diagnosis.

Very picky eating

Typical eating behaviours are common in autistic people. This could mean eating only very specific foods (often prepackaged, unchanging and non-perishable, due to these foods always tasting the same, without fail), refusing to eat foods of specific textures or colours, or refusing to let different types of food touch and 'contaminate' each other.

Inability to maintain eye contact

A main diagnostic criterion is an autistic person's inability to maintain eye contact, which then creates the sense that autistic people are more disengaged and less responsive (neither of which is correct). Eye contact can be physically and mentally painful, and forcing eye contact can impair our ability to take information in and engage with others.

Intense sensitivity to input

Sensory processing disorder is an incredibly common comorbidity with autism, causing autistic people to either be hyper (over) or hypo (under) sensitive to light, sound, taste, touch and other sensory stimuli.

Delayed movement skills

Autistic people may have a delay in fine motor skills (typically seen in children) and can have varying degrees of difficulty with these functions.

HOW AUTISM MAY APPEAR IN WOMEN

A fundamental issue of our current diagnostic criteria for autism is that the pre-existing concepts of autism are based on a predominantly male population, leaving autistic women incredibly underdiagnosed. New research is beginning to showcase what autistic women have already known for their entire lives, telling us that autism often presents incredibly differently in women, because of both our abilities to mask and our social motivation, as well as brain differences between autistic men and women.

Here is how autism may show up in women.

Reliance on other girls to guide them or speak for them

Understanding social cues can be incredibly difficult for everyone on the spectrum, but it presents a lot more in autistic women. Autistic women tend to be shy and self-aware. Because of this, and because they understand that they are different but desperately want to fit in, they often let other girls guide them, speak for them and show them how to act. They may follow others not just in their interests, but also in behaviour, which means many of us end up in sticky situations.

Passionate and limited interests

Intense special interests are a classic autistic trait regardless of gender; however, while interests for men may be more in line with science, math and trains, they often present in women as a love for animals and media and the arts, such as literature, film and music.

Masking

As mentioned, autistic females tend to be extremely socially aware, self-aware, and aware of who they're supposed to be. Thus, they may try to mimic and copy other girls to fit in better, and hide their own natural traits. This can be seen in the way they force eye contact, hold back stims, pre-prepare jokes and scripts, and mimic how others walk, dress and speak.

Broad imagination

As opposed to males on the spectrum, who can present as playing in a structured fashion, autistic females are often more imaginative when they play. This alone is a huge reason why many autistic women are never diagnosed—it seems too removed from what an autism diagnosis is 'supposed to look like'. Autistic women and girls are incredibly imaginative, often more so than their neurotypical counterparts.

Reluctance to play cooperatively

Playing make-believe was my favourite thing in the whole world (it still is), but my idea of playing wasn't exactly 'playing'; it was directing. When I played make-believe, I would script up exactly what all of the characters would do before we began and would get frustrated when someone went off script. In a way, this is the female version of the ever-so-common idea of autistic kids lining things up.

Advanced vocabulary but limited conversation

Unlike boys on the spectrum, girls rarely experience any speech or language delays. Often, we are far more advanced than our peers (and many adults!). However, communication struggles remain. Knowing how to speak to others can be hard unless it's about something we're specifically interested in—then you won't be able to shut us up.

Depression and anxiety

Autistic women are more than four times more likely to experience depression than the neurotypical population, and roughly 40 per cent of autistic women have a diagnosable anxiety disorder. There's evidence that suggests this is due to our brain structure and function, a history of social distancing, and forced masking.

Difficulty making and keeping friends

With 93 per cent of human communication being non-verbal, and because autistic people find it difficult to pick up on this communication, making friends can be hard. We are often quite clueless when it comes to making friends and sparking conversation.

Seizures

Seizures are more common in autistic females than they are in autistic males. (Ya girl has experienced *multiple* seizures at the most inconvenient times, including in the middle of a mosh pit—don't recommend it.) However, many people will grow out of them in their adult years.

Normal development but a delayed adolescence

While autistic boys tend to be diagnosed earlier in life, autistic girls often aren't diagnosed until much later. This is due to the way autism tends to present in females, and the traits are really not seen until adolescence. We tend to develop later than neurotypical girls and are more likely to be seen as incredibly youthful and naive.

AUTISM TRAITS NOT SPOKEN ABOUT

The following traits, while common in autistic people, often go unspoken about or unnoticed. They may not be listed as specific criteria in the *DSM-5* (released in 2013) but are backed up by multiple experts and research.

Sleep problems

Insomnia affects between 73 and 80 per cent of autistic individuals, and studies suggest that autistic people only spend 15 per cent of their sleep in the critical REM stage compared with around 23 per cent for neurotypical people. While we don't know the specific link between autism and sleep issues, two potential causes are sensory sensitivities and a lack of natural melatonin in our brains.

Poor and abnormal posture

Many autistic people have poor posture due to a reduced self-perception of body movement and lack of motor skills.

Different or 'odd' gait

Many autistic people have an unusual way of walking. It might be walking pigeon-toed, walking on our toes (often due to sensory issues), walking on the insides of our feet, or even having an incredibly quick walking speed. Again, this may be linked to poor perception of body movement and poor motor skills. These types of gaits may become heightened during extreme sensory sensitivity.

Connection with animals

As other humans often seem like a strange, unsettling, bizarre species to autistic people, we may find the most comfort with animals. It's no secret that the impact animals have on us can be healing and can help us to understand how to communicate. Animals don't mock, they don't pretend, they don't have hidden agendas. That sort of thing is exactly what we need ... it's what everyone needs.

Clumsiness

Autistic people can be unaware of their surroundings and are often covered in bruises. This is due to a lack of spatial awareness and poor fine-motor skills, and possibly dyspraxia, a neurological condition that is extremely common in autism. It means our hands, eyes and brains often don't link up, leaving us to be very clumsy!

Seemingly unnecessary rituals

Many of us on the spectrum have rituals that may seem odd to neurotypical viewers, appearing unnecessary and illogical (such as drinking only from a specific cup, or asking the same questions and needing a specific answer, or keeping objects in the exact same place, or playing the same way without change). But these rituals are often simply there to make us feel safe, comfortable and grounded (well and truly enough of a reason). Due to this ritualism, many autistic kids may receive a misdiagnosis of obsessive-compulsive disorder (OCD). While those who are autistic are thirteen times more likely to be diagnosed with OCD (6 per cent), there are many OCD traits that are also autism traits, without the comorbid diagnosis.

Intense compassion and empathy

There's a large expectation that autistic people inherently lack empathy and compassion. This couldn't be further from the truth and is often entirely backwards. Autistic people are some of the most compassionate, empathetic, sensitive people in the world, and can experience these emotions so deeply that they become extremely painful and overwhelming. Due to these heightened, often uncomfortable feelings, they may close off, or be too deep in their own feelings, and appear unempathetic or cold to those who don't know us or expect neurotypical emotions from a neurodivergent person.

A large and unique vocabulary

Autistic people often struggle to understand social norms and expectations, so when we learn words from books, films or whatever media we ingest, we'll use them as a part of daily conversation without considering, *Is there a simpler, shorter way of explaining this?*

It's important to add that while this can be a sign of autism, there are also many autistic people who are non-verbal or have limited vocabulary—both of which are entirely fine, and simply other elements of the spectrum!

Lack of organisation

An inability to plan and organise is a common trait for autistic individuals, thanks to our little friend 'executive dysfunction'. Planning and working out our own internal step-by-step instructions for things can be incredibly difficult.

Diagnosing ADHD

Originally, ADHD was known as 'hyperkinetic reaction of childhood' and was described in the *DSM-II* in one sentence: 'Overactivity, restlessness, distractibility, and short attention span, especially in young children; the behavior usually diminishes in adolescence.' In the 1960s, ADHD was formally recognised as a mental disorder, then it became 'attention deficit disorder with or without hyperactivity' in the 1980s.

HOW ADHD IS 'EXPECTED' TO PRESENT

These traits are expected in ADHD people and, even though they may be more in line with a male diagnostic criterion, they can still be valid for women as well.

Hyperactivity

Hyperactivity is often the number-one trait when considering an ADHD diagnosis. Typically, it is seen as an inability to sit still, consistent fidgeting, disruptiveness, excessive physical movement and excessive talking.

Impulsivity

Impulsivity is another stock-standard diagnostic criterion for ADHD, and typically means acting without thinking, interrupting, and having little perception of danger.

Self-focused behaviour

An inability to recognise other people's needs and desires (interrupting, having difficulty waiting for their turn, being impatient) is considered another typical ADHD trait.

Emotional turmoil

'Temper tantrums', as they're so painfully and wrongly called, may be common in people with ADHD, as well as emotional outbursts, an inability to control emotions and anger.

Struggles paying attention

Someone with ADHD may struggle with paying close attention to schoolwork, conversation, instructions or information, causing careless mistakes in schoolwork and social isolation.

Tendency to lose things

Keys, wallet, lunch box, schoolbag, hat, glasses . . . if it's not attached to our body, we're probably going to lose it.

Lack of follow-through on tasks and instructions

Not finishing tasks and instructions due to lack of focus or getting sidetracked is a common diagnostic criterion.

Symptoms present before age of twelve and in more than one environment

The *DSM-5* ADHD criteria insist that a diagnosis can only be made if multiple behaviours are recognised before the age of twelve and are noticed in more than one environment (that is, school and home). This is something that is problematic with women, as ADHD women often learn to mask symptoms from a young age, and therefore do not receive support or a diagnosis until our adult years.

HOW ADHD MAY APPEAR IN WOMEN

Similar to autism, women with ADHD often present differently to men with ADHD. We are master maskers, are taught to comply, and often showcase inattentiveness, hyperactivity and impulsiveness in ways that aren't seen as socially disruptive as they are in males with ADHD. Here is how ADHD may present in women.

Inattentiveness

While boys with ADHD may present externalised behaviours, such as impulsivity and hyperactivity, girls may experience ADHD in a more internalised way—inattention being a huge one. Not paying attention to the task at hand and becoming easily distracted can be huge barriers for girls with ADHD. They often lead to exclusion and forgetfulness.

Hyper-focus as compensation

To compensate for inattentiveness, girls with ADHD are often incredibly good at hyper-focusing on something we like or are good at. We'll put so much energy and effort into this one thing—whether that's sport, music, a television series or something else—and focus so intently on it that people often dismiss the possibility of ADHD and attribute our behaviour to defiance or laziness. ('She can't have ADHD, she pays attention when she wants to.')

Constant motion

Being constantly on the move doesn't necessarily mean the stereotypical 'bouncing off the walls' that ADHD is known for. Often, it's in smaller, more subtle ways, largely due to the fact that, while we need to release energy, we are aware of the social factors causing silent judgements to be constantly cast in our direction. So, we'll find ways to move that don't draw as much attention. Constantly fidgeting, tapping fingers, doodling, jiggling a leg—these are tiny, somewhat subtle ways to release built-up energy and find a sense of grounding (otherwise known as stimming).

Difficulty making friends

Friendship can be hard for anyone, but if you're a neurodivergent girl, that difficulty level just went up tenfold. A girl with ADHD is often impulsive, hyperactive and forgetful, making the little complex nuances of female friendships more difficult.

Messiness

This can be for a number of reasons, including poor working memory, which makes it hard to visualise and plan the process of cleaning. I'll get distracted by my dog barking, or seeing my fish tank and remembering I need to feed the fish, or my jewellery box that needs reorganising. I then completely forget the task of cleaning in the first place.

Messiness doesn't just stay within the house, though. Messiness in all situations can be an indication of ADHD. Messiness with food, with schoolwork, with writing, with your purse or backpack. If there's a mess to be made, rest assured we'll find a way to make it.

Low self-esteem

The struggle with friendships can lead to feelings of low self-esteem and anxiety. Girls with ADHD are likely to blame themselves in many situations. As an example, if a boy with ADHD fails a test, he is more likely to say the test was simply too difficult, whereas girls with ADHD are more likely to see their failure as a sign that they're 'not smart enough'.

When it comes to social situations, and life in general, girls with ADHD tend to be a lot more self-aware than their male counterparts. We usually know why we find life hard, but we don't know how to change it, resulting in feelings of anxiety and low self-esteem.

Mental health issues

Girls with ADHD are three times more likely to struggle from eating disorders, depression, anxiety and substance disorders than neurotypical girls. Ten per cent of women with ADHD are also diagnosed with depression, and 38 per cent meet the criteria for an anxiety disorder.

Daydreaming

While boys with ADHD may be more inclined to be physically energetic, this energy often presents itself as daydreaming for girls. For example, a boy with ADHD may feel the need to fidget and move and jump out of his chair, but a girl may doodle images she sees in her mind or stare out the window. This endless daydreaming often gets us into trouble, such as missing important social cues, instructions or assignments. But it can also be our greatest superpower—some of the world's greatest artists and creators have ADHD and are often dreamers.

Chattiness

Hyperactivity and impulsivity may manifest verbally in women, as opposed to the usual physical signs in men. ADHD girls are also often highly emotional, unable to slow their thoughts down, and struggle to process their feelings, giving us a tendency to overshare and over chat. Our struggle with social cues can also mean that we sometimes talk out of turn or out of place, which, again, leads to difficulty with friends.

People with ADHD also have a tendency to speak extremely fast. I talk like a cheetah on steroids, and regularly find myself putting videos and podcasts on double speed to overcome the pauses most people put between their words.

Poor decision-making skills

Decision-making is a massive challenge for people with ADHD. Girls with ADHD may freeze up and be unable to filter out options to come to the correct or desired decision. Distraction, daydreaming and the endless possibilities and scenarios that we come up with can all be reasons for this. We also often struggle to prioritise, and all options may seem equally important or significant. This can lead to poor or impulsive decisions.

ADHD TRAITS NOT SPOKEN ABOUT

There are common traits within ADHD individuals that often not spoken about, or they go unnoticed due to the silence around them. These may not be listed as specific *DSM* criteria but much of this information is from experts, backed by lived experience.

Hyper-focus

When most of us think of ADHD, we think of someone being 'unfocused'. It's one of the primary traits we've come to correlate with ADHD. However, sometimes this couldn't be further from the truth. In fact, ADHD individuals have such intense focus that there's a term for it: 'hyper-focus'. This happens when our minds fixate on one thing for extended periods of time, to the point where it can become quite difficult to do anything else.

It can become difficult for us to switch over our thinking and, due to this, we may lose track of time, forget to do basic tasks (including eating and personal care), and miss important cues and information.

Time-management issues

ADHD individuals see and experience time differently from those who are neurotypical. We're often unable to anticipate future rewards and consequences, have an utterly godlike ability to procrastinate, have minimal ability to establish a level of importance, and struggle with being able to coordinate, organise and format our days, plans and routines. All of this goes back to poor executive functioning. This leaves us with a warped sense of time, with things often forgotten, or realised too late.

Rejection dysphoria

Up to 99 per cent of people with ADHD are more sensitive to rejection than neurotypical people, and one in three will say it's the most difficult part of being ADHD.

With rejection dysphoria, the feeling of criticism or rejection (whether literal or just something that we believe or feel) can become so intense that it takes over our entire beings. This can lead to depression, self-esteem issues and social withdrawal.

Sleep problems

More than 67 per cent of people with ADHD struggle with sleep issues. These problems may stem from impaired alertness and regulation circuits in the brain. Or the fact that we often struggle to keep a schedule and 'factor in' sleep due to our inability to prioritise. Or because many people with ADHD have comorbid conditions that make sleep difficult, such as restless legs syndrome or apnoea.

When the world is quiet and there's nothing for our brain to fixate on, it finds its own things to get busy about. We have an inability to shut off our minds. When we're tired, ADHD symptoms get worse, and sleeping gets harder, which makes us tired, and the cycle continues.

Intense emotions

People with ADHD often experience intense emotions. Working memory impairments allow momentary emotions to become too strong, flooding the brain with that one intense emotion. We'll often also fixate on the current emotion that we're feeling, and it can take over our entire being.

Low tolerance for boredom

ADHD folk intensely crave constant stimuli. It's why we get fixated on tasks. It's why we struggle to sleep. It's why we stim. So, boredom can actually become physically and emotionally distressing, and leave people with ADHD feeling anxious and on edge.

While rest, silence and relaxation may be the dream for some, for many people with ADHD this can feel like a prison.

Impulsive shopping

Similar to hyperactivity, impulsivity is almost a given with ADHD. But while impulsivity is often expected to present as interrupting others and doing things without thinking, it can show up more subtly, most commonly as impulsive shopping. While this is due to our impulsive habits, it can also be a quick hit of dopamine, the feel-good hormone, something those of us with ADHD constantly crave.

Poor working memory

While our long-term memories are usually pretty groovy (often even better than those of neurotypical people—we'll remember everything, and probably panic about something small that happened years ago and has been long forgotten by the entirety of the planet minus us), our short-term or working memory is often not so good.

We may have difficulty remembering assignments or completing tasks. We're thinking so much and so constantly that often, instead of all the tabs in our brains being open simultaneously, one thought will push the others away, and they disappear.

Object permanence issues

As with our poor working memory, our brains require focus, even if subconsciously, to remember tasks and objects. With so much stimuli always entering our brain, sometimes our brain kicks out items temporarily, to the point of them disappearing from our plane of existence. A closed computer tab to be looked at later will never be opened again. Vegetables in the crisper will go mouldy because we can't see them. Clothes at the back of our wardrobes will remain unworn. This goes beyond objects and chores; it can also extend to people! Out of sight, out of mind.

Bursts of motivation based on interest

Many people with ADHD are criticised for lacking motivation, or scolded for only wanting to do 'fun tasks'. We may excel at our favourite subjects in school and spend hours on them, but we may become entirely unmotivated and unfocused on things we don't really enjoy.

When we're doing something we love, our brain rewards us with happy chemicals. Our entire brain chemistry changes when we're engaged in tasks that we find rewarding, and it's our brain chemistry that sustains our focus and attention.

Challenging the labels

Despite Asperger's syndrome being the label typed onto my diagnostic sheet by a psychologist when I was thirteen years old, you'll notice I don't use that term anywhere else in this book. Instead, I refer to myself as 'autistic'. Asperger's syndrome was considered a correct diagnosis and has been widely accepted and identified within the community since 1994. But one of the best parts of our world is accepting and embracing growth and change when new information is presented to us. The term 'Asperger's syndrome' is no longer considered a diagnosis, and within the latest *DSM-5* criteria (which still have many faults) the traits identifying the condition are now listed as 'autism'.

There are many, many reasons why I and so many others have pulled away from the term. But the one reason that the majority of people have yet to learn about—and the most shocking—is that Hans Asperger, the 'inventor' of the term, was a Nazi who assisted in the murder of disabled children during the Second World War.

Asperger, an Austrian paediatrician, was for many decades recognised as a pioneer in the study of autism. To some, he was even deemed a hero, rescuing groups of autistic children from the Nazi extermination program. He did this by emphasising the intelligence of some autistic children, describing them as having 'high-functioning autism' (another feral term that we will get to later—*one atrocity at a time, please*). However, after an eight-year-long study that was released in 2018, we now have indisputable evidence that Asperger assisted in the murder of disabled children, including those who were autistic.

Conducting Nazi ideological-based research on autistic children, Asperger came to the conclusion that some of the children had higher IQs and were deemed worthy of survival. He narcissistically coined the term 'Asperger's syndrome' to differentiate and separate them from other autistic children. That same research described autism as a 'psychopathic, schizophrenic disorder', and the children he tested under this were categorised as unsocial, undesirable and low functioning.

Those not lucky enough to fall under his new 'high-functioning' label were sent to a clinic called Am Spiegelgrund, a place that Asperger both published papers on and spoke about publicly. Here, these children that he didn't deem worthy of survival were experimented on, starved and put to death.

Nearly 800 children were murdered under Hans Asperger's watch.

So, why are we still so set on using a term coined by a murderer? Especially when it has been proven time and time again that his research was complete and utter hogwash and holds no value within our modern-day understanding of what autism *really* is?

Asperger's syndrome, as we know it today, has absolutely no correlation to Hans Asperger's research and, yet, we are still so determined to name an entire group of individuals after the man who assisted in the knowing murder of people like me. And, as important, we, as a society, must not accept that one group of people is deemed worthy, while another is not—despite there being absolutely no difference between them other than how their minds work. Consider the social implications that ideology has on both the autistic community and society as a whole.

I hear you thinking, *Okay, so we'll stop using Asperger's syndrome. We'll use functioning labels instead!*

Wrong. Equally as harmful.

You can't use a new word to replace an old one without it holding the exact same correlation, segregation and complacency that the original term was associated with. Instead of the 1930s' mindset of *People with Asperger's are worthy of survival, but those who have autism are not*, we now see a twenty-first century version of that: *People who are high functioning are worthy of survival, but those who are low functioning*... It's just a more modernised, accepted vocabulary. Instead of 'worthy of survival', our new language is being 'worthy' in capitalism and 'worthy' of support.

Functioning labels were created by non-autistic people who know very little about autism, who have no connection with autism,

We, as a society, must not accept that one group of people is deemed worthy, while another is not.

and who want to make it easier for the neurotypical community to understand our minds by further alienating us. They're used to telling now one entire group that they're incapable, and another group that their struggles are minimal and do not matter. Both of those are incredibly problematic, outdated ways of thinking. And, again, both link back directly to Hans Asperger's Nazi ideologies.

Functioning labels and Asperger's syndrome both need to be erased entirely from diagnostic criteria and our vocabulary if we want any chance of a more equal future. They only serve to segregate, label and ultimately harm us. Our minds are deemed different and confusing to *you*, therefore you need to box us in a way that makes sense to *you*, at the expense of our wellbeing. This has occurred despite 'functioning labels' not actually existing in diagnostic tools and holding no scientific merit.

Plainly and simply: functioning labels do not exist. They cannot exist. Functioning labels have never helped autistic people, and we need to call them out for what they are: *Is this person capable of producing capitalistic value, or not?* That's the real reason these labels are used, often hidden behind the idea of providing support, but it's false support.

'But, Chloé,' I hear you say, 'we need to establish a person's level of functioning so we know what their support needs are! So we know if they can live independently! So we know if they can . . . function.'

I hear you. But, alas—wrong.

One autistic person's 'level of functioning' will fluctuate throughout their day, week and life, depending upon circumstances, environment, mood and other factors. Someone who has been deemed 'high functioning' simply due to external factors (such as their home life, their support circle, or simply how well they have learned to mask themselves) may in fact need more resources and support than someone who has been deemed 'low functioning'.

Likewise, our understanding of functioning labels does not help the autistic person but does allow the labeller to pin something on them.

People who are deemed to be at one end of the spectrum are seen as incapable. They aren't given the respect that they deserve, and the things that they *can* do are overlooked. We see someone who outwardly presents a certain way, and immediately pin them as low functioning—this is particularly true of people who may be non- or partially verbal. By calling someone low functioning for not using words, you're invalidating their ability to communicate in their way. (If you ask me, that doesn't make *them* the ones who are low functioning, when the people around them are the ones unable to understand.) These people will only ever be seen as what they are not. A label of 'low functioning' denies the person the ability to thrive in their own way in their own time.

On the flip side, those on the other end of the spectrum may simply be seen as 'quirky', and their struggles are diminished and overlooked.

Just as you wouldn't label a neurotypical person as low- or high-functioning, it makes zero sense to do it with autistic people. As with everyone, our struggles and strengths are our own individual struggles and strengths.

Autism *is* a spectrum, and it is this wording that has led people into believing that that must mean there is a low end and a high end on the spectrum.

'You must be very low on the spectrum then.'
'He's more autistic than you; he's very high up on the spectrum.'

This language is also used by neurotypical people to push themselves into our narrative: 'Oh, autism is a spectrum! And everyone is on it!' But this is incredibly problematic.

Autism is not a linear spectrum; it is not a singular line where one end is 'a little bit autistic' and the other is 'very autistic'. Instead, the autism spectrum is more like a colour wheel, in which every colour represents a different strength, a different struggle, a different identity, but all of the colours are autism. Every autistic person is their own, individual, different colour code. No colour is more or less colourful than another colour—they are all equally important parts of the palette. (And, likewise, if you are not autistic, you are not on this palette.)

Instead of trying to give someone a made-up label that's designed to help the viewer, it's paramount that we start to focus on providing care and support on an individual, case-by-case basis.

There are many autistic people who were once diagnosed with either Asperger's syndrome or high-functioning autism and they cling on to that diagnosis with everything they have. They will fight to the end that these are words *they* identify with, and they shouldn't have to conform to being labelled as autistic. And I understand this.

Asperger's supremacy and internalised ableism are things that are still so pervasive within our community. I know, because Asperger's was an instrumental part of my online identity for eight years, and when the time came to change and step away from it, it was really, really difficult. Change is terrifying, especially when that change means losing a label that has been protecting you.

But why are we letting a man who wanted us gone from the planet to be such a crucial part of our lives?

Why are we still allowing him to decide which of us are deemed worthy, when worth and value have never been depicted by a label?

I genuinely believe that our world is moving in a more positive direction and that good will always win. But it's important that we work together to educate and ensure that the good outweighs the bad, and that we continue to create a better world for all of us.

For my entire teenage life, I had understood that my brain was wrong, and weird, and strange because of what fearmongering-based videos and articles told me, and because of how people were treating me, and because of how our world as a whole sees autism. But we desperately, desperately need to change that. We need to change our outlook on the different, because we've suffered for far too long.

Moving beyond fear

We human beings label things, it's what we do. It's how our little pea brains make sense of a world that has no order. Even before a diagnosis of autism or ADHD or whatever it may be, a neurodivergent person will be labelled as weird, quirky, different, strange, unusual . . . 'not supposed to be here'—labels that were put on us from the moment society made us believe we were wrong for being different. Replacing these negative, confusing labels with one simple label of 'autism', changes everything. It becomes a positive identity that we can finally make sense of.

If you are neurotypical, make a genuine effort to understand neurodiversity—not from fearmongering 'professionals' who don't actually speak for us, but from neurodivergent people themselves, who are sick and tired of having their voices, their identity and their lives taken away from them. If you're reading this book, congratulations, you're off to a cracking start.

If you are neurodivergent . . . I know it's hard. I understand that neurodivergence in a neurotypical-pleasing society can be terrifying, and difficult, and confusing, but it is time that you embraced your neurodiversity, it is time that you embraced who you are. Who you are is exactly who you're supposed to be, and the sooner you learn to embrace that, the sooner you can step into the next chapter of your fairytale.

Getting a diagnosis never changed who I was. I had always been neurodivergent, and I always will be neurodivergent. So, in some ways, those words on that piece of paper that gave me an official, clinical name for myself didn't *really* change anything.

But in other ways, it changed the world.

Because now I understood who I was. Now, I had a better understanding that this weird, strange, crazy roller coaster that I was on wasn't a solo ride. I was now able to seek resources, and find community groups, and grow a deeper understanding of who I was. I was now able to see myself for the human I was, instead of the human I could never be.

Elsa's ice powers in *Frozen* scared her once, but they became her greatest power.

Vanellope von Schweetz's glitch in *Wreck-It Ralph* once brought her uncertainty, but then it became her most powerful asset.

Meilin Lee feared her red panda ancestors in *Turning Red*, but discovered her true, unmasked self after embracing them.

You, in all that you are, are your greatest power. Diagnosis and all.

At twenty-two, I was diagnosed with ADHD (again, looking back, I don't know how it took so long). This time, instead of being fearful of a new diagnosis, I went into it with an open mind and kindness and love for myself and my mind. For nothing had changed, except for the fact that I now had an even better opportunity to embrace, love and care for my mind in the way that it individually needs.

I am who I am—regardless of diagnosis, words, labels.

My mind is brilliant, and it's time that I start seeing that.

Now I know that I'm not *Chloé: weirdly, devastatingly, ruined by autism.*

I am *Chloé; weirdly, wonderfully, beautifully autistic and ADHD.* And that is exactly who I am supposed to be.

WHAT TO DO AFTER YOUR DIAGNOSIS

Fellow humans (and anyone who feels they have come from an alien planet), don't fear a diagnosis, don't fear a change that was never really a change at all, but merely the writing of a title of an important part of your story. If you believe there's a sparkle in you, don't fear it, but instead take that step forward and embrace it. So . . .

Research

Whether a diagnosis was a long time coming, or it was something that came as a complete surprise to you, a new understanding of your identity can be daunting without the right support and research. Speak to your healthcare team to see what further information they can give you. Read books and watch videos. We live in a world where information is more accessible than ever, so use that to your advantage. Become an expert on you!

Find support groups

Finding support groups was such a crucial step in my own journey, and one in which I was able to truly find my first sidekicks. Autism-based support groups—a whole group of others just like me—helped me realise that if I *had* landed on an alien planet, there were a lot of others in the same rocket ship.

For the first time in my life, I felt safe, I felt accepted, I felt like I had a community that was built for me.

Allow yourself to be neurodivergent

It's both common and expected for your 'neurodivergent traits' to become more obvious after a diagnosis. It's not because you're projecting. It's not because you're trying to prove anything. It's not because you're faking it to meet the standards of a new diagnosis. It's because you've been taught to mask these traits for your entire life, and for the first time you have an explanation and a reason for them.

Accept yourself

It can be hard to be neurodivergent in a neurotypical world, but the sooner you come to a positive understanding of your mind, and accept who you are, the quicker you're going to be able to step into the next chapter of your fairytale.

FOR PARENTS AND CARERS: WHAT TO DO AFTER YOUR CHILD'S DIAGNOSIS

Thanks to media, fearmongering and stereotypes, autism is portrayed as a terrifying, life-altering condition that will radically change your family's dynamic. Parents often become fearful, sad and anxious. They can also go into denial or feel desperate for a 'cure'. You don't have to give in to those thoughts and feelings. Instead, this is what you *should* do after your child receives a diagnosis.

Tell them!

Parents, when your child receives a diagnosis, for goodness' sake, tell them. Children *know* that they're neurodivergent. They *know* that they're different. I promise you that a label of autism, or ADHD, or whatever it may be is far better than the labels they have internally given themselves.

Accept the diagnosis

Your child is neurodivergent, nothing will ever change that (no, nothing). So, stop googling it, stop asking your Facebook groups' opinions, stop trying fad diets and yoga stretches. What you can change is the way you perceive disability. These are the cards that you and your child have been dealt, so play them.

Listen

Listening is not just something reserved for your ears—it's for your heart, your eyes, your actions. Listen to your child's sensory needs. Learn the difference between meltdowns and tantrums. Listen to their special interests and encourage them with everything you have. Listen when they're struggling, listen when they're glowing.

Speak up for your child, but do not speak over your child

Every child needs a superhero, a sidekick, a person who has their back no matter what. But there is a difference between being that person and taking away your child's voice.

This may be incredibly difficult for some people to grasp, but your child's diagnosis is not about you. There is nothing more frustrating than seeing people wearing stereotypical puzzle-piece T-shirts and captioning their Facebook statuses with 'God gives the hardest battles to the strongest people'. *Lord almighty; shut up.*

I understand that it's difficult; parenting as a whole is difficult. But if you're struggling as a bystander, imagine how your child is feeling. Be a voice for your child, but do not be your child's voice.

Listen to the community for advice

It's only natural to seek support and advice but look beyond professionals with nicely framed certificates and bookshelves of fancy

Listening is not just something reserved for your ears—it's for your heart, your eyes, your actions.

textbooks (which I can promise you were not written by anyone who has ever personally lived it!). Look to the community that your child is a part of. Listen to autistic adults, listen to ADHD adults, listen to parents who have been on this journey and know it so much better than anyone else ever will.

Focus on your child's strengths

Everyone has different strengths and weaknesses, neurodivergent or not. The most important thing that you can do is focus on your child's strengths. They already know their struggles, they already know their differences, they don't need you to bring awareness to them, too. Focus on your child's strengths, their special interests, and the things they're good at.

Not only are they going to flourish, but it's going to completely reshape the way they see their diagnosis and themselves. Instead of thinking, *I can't do this because I'm autistic*, the language will change to, *I can do this because I'm autistic.*

Love your child unconditionally

Every child deserves to be loved. Every child deserves to know that who they are is okay. And every child deserves to feel that from the adults in their lives. It is so incredibly difficult to love ourselves when we know that the grown-ups supporting us don't. (And I promise you, it doesn't matter how good of a poker face you have, children know.)

Be gentle with yourself, and with your child

There is no instruction book to parenting. At least as far as I know—my biggest responsibility in life is still only a blind axolotl.

No one is expecting you to be the perfect parent. No one is expecting you to have all of the answers. No one is expecting you to change the world with your parenting or get it right all the time. Be gentle with yourself and understand that it's okay to get things wrong sometimes. It's okay to not fully know what you're doing. As long as there's love, respect and a drive to continue towards a better, more understanding future, you're doing okay. The rest will fall into place.

Find support groups

All of us need support to grow, to thrive, and to simply survive. And when your situation is not typical, the need for support increases. Specific support groups are everywhere, both in person and online, and finding one that works for you can be a crucial part of your journey.

Do not hide a diagnosis

Your child knows that they're different. *They know that they're different.* Hiding a child's diagnosis doesn't protect them, it creates further segregation, fear and loneliness.

Instead, embrace the diagnosis. Find people within their special interests and talents who have the same diagnosis (there'll be a bunch of us and we're bloody cool, I promise you). Praise their incredible brain and remind them that who they are is exactly who they're supposed to be. You're not protecting them from a diagnosis, you're stopping them from discovering their identity.

Don't try to change your child; change your mindset

Your child is neurodivergent. Nothing will ever change that. And it's vital that you accept that, for your wellbeing and for theirs.

Show them compassion, show them love, show them understanding. Protect them from the evils of the world, but don't hide them from it. Teach them to love and to be loved. Teach them to value and to be valued. Teach them all that they are. Remind yourself and them that who they are is exactly who they're supposed to be.

It's not the child who needs to change, it's the world. And you as their parent have the ability to spark that change.

CHAPTER 7

Settling into Who You Are

'Normality' has never been achievable for me. I spent so many years desperately trying to be someone I could never be, and became a master of disguise in the process, learning to be the 'perfect normal'. I masked, I pretended, I played the part that was expected. I moulded my mind, my personality, my entire being to become someone society would praise me for . . . or, at the very least, not hurt me for.

Oddly enough, it didn't work.

Instead of becoming 'normal', I became a shell of the girl I had once been. I never gained normality, I merely lost myself in the disguise.

Truly settling into who you are is one of the greatest things any of us can do, and it is also often the most difficult. And when you're neurodivergent, it's a whole new ballgame.

When you spend your days trying to be someone you never can be and are ridiculed for the small parts of the real, authentic you that you do accidentally reveal, you begin to lose all understanding of who you really are. Like a lost ancient language, like a neglected instrument, like hardened paint pots, when things are not in use, they die off, they're forgotten, they solidify. When you cannot be your true self for fear of what might happen if you do, the real you begins to fade.

During the years leading up to my diagnosis, I had started to lose all parts of Chloé, and I could see genuine fear and worry in my parents' faces when I declined suggestions of things that had once brought me joy. When my smile had faded. When I was no longer the Chloé who would exuberantly and loudly announce my new-found facts to anyone who would or wouldn't listen, or stand on top of a table at La Porchetta to sing 'God Help the Outcasts', or happily befriend snails and baby birds instead of children her own age. I had become broken, quiet and still. Chloé Hayden, in all that she had been, was disappearing. Left in her place was the shell of a failed perfect version of normal.

This was a time in my life when I didn't believe there was a light at the end of the tunnel. When I thought my fairytale had failed and that there was no point in continuing to turn the pages to see where it might go. When I thought that there were no further chapters to be written. But, if Disney has taught me anything, it's that if we think the end is coming but we haven't yet reached our Happily Ever After, we are still in our dragon-fighting Adventure stage. We still have pages to turn, we still have chapters to live.

And, like a newly freed genie, like a lion cub going back to his homeland, like an ice queen coming to understand her powers, it takes time after leaving scary, uncomfortable environments to find your feet and rediscover the person you are. For that shell to fill again with the soul of the human you always have been but have been hiding away for far too long. But trust me: as in every fairytale, your dragons can be slain, your chapters can continue, and your life can, and will, have a Happily Ever After.

Being seen as 'less than'

Identity is one of the most important aspects of being human. It is a sense of self, the little puzzle pieces that make us who we are—gender, values, moral beliefs, race, ethnicity, religion, disability, age and every other tiny aspect of you. Identity plays an incredibly significant part in how we see, interact with, understand and experience the world around us, as well as shaping the challenges we face and the opportunities we have. Our identities make us who we are, and all aspects of our identities are important, including (maybe even specifically) our disabilities.

Our identities make us who we are, and all aspects of our identities are important, including (maybe even specifically) our disabilities.

Despite the importance that difference holds in our lives, it can be incredibly difficult to come to terms with that difference when it is a disability, and to see the positives of it. This is due to ableism, which is discrimination against neurodivergent and disabled people in favour of neurotypical, able-bodied people. Ableism can be both externalised and internalised, and is something that all of us, disabled or not, experience, see and use. It's something that has been bred into the core of our being, and our entire social system and culture.

Historically, disability has always and disappointingly been synonymous with 'bad'. We've been socialised to hear the word 'disabled' and automatically associate it with being inferior, wrong, defective. The prefix 'dis' *means* the negative of the root word. This creates a 'deficit framework' of disability, and it means that the experience we hold of disability is one of sadness, loss and negativity, where those of us who are disabled are often seen as less valuable, less human. This makes it so incredibly difficult for those of us who are disabled to form a positive identity.

I can't count the number of times that I've been approached by parents who have asked me when the correct time to tell their child that they're autistic is. Or to express concern that a diagnosis is going to further isolate their child. I can't count the number of times that a grown man has angrily told me I have no right to be so openly positive about my disability, because it's going to give the wrong idea to other autistic children that they should be proud of their condition. Or that a mum has sobbed to me because she's just discovered her child is autistic, or a father has angrily told me that I'm wrong for saying his child will never outgrow their autism, or a so-called therapist has given me a dumbed-down story about how we need to not normalise autism and disabilities and difference.

Daily, I get messages that invalidate me as a human because I'm autistic, with people asking me why I would ever be proud of something like that. Daily, I see, hear and experience people try to diminish my identity, and refuse to acknowledge the identity of their children, their patients, their students. When I look at the world around me, I'm reminded by the media, by politicians, by the very essence of our culture that my mind is wrong, that I'm not needed, that neurodivergence as a whole is indisputably delinquent, and that our identities are not considered important or whole.

Our society is run on a deficit/medical framework, which presents the idea that failure, lack of achievement and lack of 'normality' are a product of the individual, and that consequently, some people are deficit by nature. This model doesn't allow people to function the way they are able because it refuses to accommodate differences. Examples of a disability deficit framework include:

- a teacher refusing to offer worksheets in a larger font for a visually impaired student; this student is therefore unable to learn the material
- classrooms not allowing autistic students the sensory tools they may need to cope with the environment; these students are then unable to participate in class and learn
- no ramps into buildings, making them inaccessible to wheelchair users and those otherwise physically disabled, creating restrictions and leaving groups of people unable to participate.

A social/diversity framework, on the other hand, presents disability as simply a variation from the typical; not to be seen as bad or negative, but another natural aspect of human existence. This framework believes that the problem isn't in the person, but in the environment, in social barriers and in the education system.

This framework draws on the thinking of disabled people and supports an all-inclusive society and education, believing that disability isn't because of the individual, but because of the way society is organised. When barriers are removed, disabled people have the opportunity to be equal in society. Examples of a social/diversity framework include:

★ teachers providing classroom handouts in a variety of formats (large print, a tablet with text-to-speech, and so on), so students are able to read and learn in the way that is best suited to them—this will mean that no student is worse or better off than another because or in spite of their needs
★ classrooms being stocked with the tools students need in order to cope (weighted blankets, fidget toys, noise-cancelling headphones, a separate 'quiet' room for students to go to when they're distressed or in sensory overload) in environments that may otherwise be stressful, as this better supports students to learn and interact
★ wheelchair-accessible ramps and lifts being put in all the places there are stairs so that wheelchair users and otherwise physically disabled people will no longer be functionally disabled.

Overall, a change in attitude towards a social/diversity framework would mean that those with a disability would no longer be seen as having an impairment. Instead, they would be seen as simply having a different way of functioning and welcomed in all areas of society.

Currently, many people—autistic, neurodivergent, disabled or otherwise marginalised—go their entire lives undiagnosed, unheard and hidden in our communities due to the deficit/medical framework. It is why disabled people are so lacking in resources and accommodation despite a world that is more than capable of providing them. It's why I am so adamantly against person-first labels (person *with* autism, person *with* a disability) that announce disabilities like they're something separate from us, like they're something that can be removed. It's why I'm so passionately for identity-first labels (autistic person, disabled person) that validate, value and affirm a disabled person's identity in all that they *are*.

The person-first logic is why parents are so goddamn terrified to reveal to their children a key part of their identity, and why poor mental health rates, death by suicide and overall exclusion is higher in disabled people than in the typical community. It is why autistic people in Australia have a twenty-six-year shorter life expectancy. It is why marginalised groups of every type fear the concept of being different, and why the world can be such a terrifying place for us. It is why a positive identity is so, so important, not just for disabled people, but for everyone. It stems outwards into every aspect of society.

No one can truly be who they're supposed to be until society allows us *all* to be ourselves.

Confronting the negative after a diagnosis

I think there's another bit of a misconception that comes with receiving a diagnosis. Apart from the negative connotations of disability, there is also the expectation that a diagnosis will bring an immediate sense of relief, joy and understanding, like you've been given a reason for who you are and, therefore, it all makes sense. In some ways that may be true but it's so much deeper than that.

For me, yes, I now had a name that answered many questions, but that same name cracked open new feelings and avenues and, in some ways, left me feeling just as much of an outcast—if not more. This was because society had taught me that my identity was not okay.

From the moment you type in 'autism', 'ADHD', or any form of neurological or physical difference into the search bars of the internet, the first things that pop up showcase our society's disdain for anyone who presents differently.

Will autism ever go away?
Can autism ever be cured?
How to cure autism at home
Can autistic people become normal?

Further into your search, you come across Facebook pages with parents sharing tips on how to cure autistic children—everything from essential oils to invasive, traumatic therapy. Or parents angry with their children, with themselves, with God for bringing an autistic child into their lives. You'll also find news articles explaining how we can rid our society of disability. How Iceland, Denmark and France have almost completely wiped out babies born with Down's syndrome due to genetic testing and pregnancy termination, and that the largest autism organisation is funding research to do the same thing for autistic people. And, in the United Kingdom, if you're autistic or have other neurological or learning disorders and contract Covid-19, you will automatically, non-consensually, be put on a do not resuscitate (DNR) order. You'll also find bullying and anti-disabled language on children's gaming servers, where young children learn to use words like 'autism' and 'retard' when they're trash-talking their friends.

CHANGE THE LANGUAGE YOU USE

All of us use, or have used, disability-deficit language—it's ingrained into us as a society. If you've used words such as 'crazy', 'moron', 'idiot', 'hysterical', 'nuts', 'imbecile' or 'spaz', you've partaken (albeit, likely unknowingly) in ableist, derogatory, disability-deficit language. These words were once used medically to categorise disabled and mentally ill people, marking them as less human. They were widespread terms in medical textbooks and scientific journals and used to support eugenic practices, including forced sterilisation and institutionalisation. The casual use of these words continues to foster comfort in how our society marginalises and harms disabled people and their use should be stopped.

Instead of using this:	**Use this:**
Retarded, stupid	frustrating, annoying, irritating
spaz	silly, dorky, cheesy, nonsensical
crazy	intense, awesome, amazing, wild
lame	bad, awful, annoying
psychotic	dangerous, menacing, threatening
autistic	annoying, foolish, strange
cripple	injured, hurt

Likewise, when we're using disability and mental health terms as adjectives, it continues to push wrong ideas on disability, neurodiversity and mental health, leaving those who are actually diagnosed to feel further stigmatised, open to stereotypes and less support.

Stop using:	**When you mean:**
ADHD	distracted
OCD	organised
autistic	strange
depressed	sad
anorexic	skinny
traumatic	inconvenient
bipolar	moody
triggered	upset, offended

After receiving a diagnosis, the minimal resources that we may be linked to (if we're lucky) are for the benefit of parents, carers and those who are third-party viewers, rather than *for neurodivergent people*. We're given books that have been created by doctors and psychologists and neurologists who may have studied our brains for a number of years and can spit out information until the cows come home. But, assuming they are neurotypical, they have never and will never experience or understand what it feels like to have our minds. We're given clinical books and clinical videos, and are taught as soon as the new label is attached to us that it's a cold, medical, distant thing, like our brains are no longer ours.

And, when we try to rid ourselves of these views and do our own research in an attempt to find things that feel closer to home and less analytical and impersonal, we are led to articles, sob stories and posts that highlight the disappointment, fear and sorrow that surround all aspects of us, making us feel further invalidated, segregated and alienated.

We're then told by those close to us that they're 'so sorry' about our 'situation' or that they 'can't be friends with us anymore'. When I was first diagnosed, I lost countless so-called friends after telling them. People who had been close to me for years and had eventually come out and told me that they couldn't handle the stigma and side-eyes from their other friends if they hung out with an autistic person. I've had friends physically put a hand over my mouth when I questioned them on this, shushing me and saying my diagnosis wasn't something to be proud of, that if I knew what was good for me I'd keep my mouth shut about it. Within my closer circle, many people denied my diagnosis—family members told me my diagnosis was wrong, that I was 'normal'.

How can we possibly find love and sanctuary in our identities when the entire world has taught us that these identities are unwanted? It's why many of us mask ourselves, disguise ourselves, become people we are not, to simply survive. But, when we wear the mask long enough, when we hide our own self for long enough, and when we allow these incorrect and damaging frameworks to infiltrate our brains, we may be left uncertain about our identities, and invalidated in who we are. Many of us feel like impostors in our own skin.

Autistic people, particularly women, are impeccable maskers. We're chameleons, we'll hide our true identities for our entire lives for fear of being ridiculed, bullied or otherwise cast out because we are different. This masking becomes such a key part of our new, false identity that when we truly do discover who we are, and choose to openly be that person, we can often be left with questions like, *Perhaps I'm just faking it?* Or, *If I was able to play pretend for this long, maybe it wasn't actually pretend.* Or, *I'm not autistic enough.*

We read about stereotyped, untrue 'diagnostic criteria' for neurodivergent minds, have societal expectations stuck in our heads, or see neurodiversity poorly represented in the media and it becomes difficult to separate truth from fiction. We feel pressure to be a certain way as a neurodivergent human in a neurotypical world.

The neurotypical world can be relentless, and rough, and unforgiving. It has shown me time and time again, from the moment I gained consciousness that it was a world not built for me, that it didn't value me for who I was, before or after a diagnosis. I so easily could have allowed those unmet expectations and understandings to swallow me whole like Pinocchio inside the whale—for a long time, I almost did.

But, over time, and with the right resources, and the right groups, and the right people surrounding us, with steps taken to claim our identities, rather than be fearful of them, we can allow the chapters of embracing those identities to begin.

We can allow our fairytales to continue.

We can defeat the dragons.

Turning the page to a new chapter

My diagnosis, the switch to homeschooling, and the beginning of me discovering my true identity and allowing myself to open up to the world were a whirlwind of extreme events mashed into a short chapter of my life. Once I was out of the toxic schoolyard environment where I had to hide myself away, I finally had the chance to learn who I could be, to discover myself.

A part of my at-home study was being able to go out into the community for my education, instead of sitting in a classroom with a pen in one hand and a textbook in the other. I wasn't overly terrified of people when it was in settings that made sense to me. I had previously worked at my local riding school as a kid and had never felt more at home. And most Fridays, for as long as I could remember, were spent with my grandparents, Nanny and Kenpa, at their house for 'Train Day', when Kenpa's friends would all come over to build and marvel at the life-sized train that circled his property and I'd chat happily to men sixty years my senior. So, taking a leap of faith into the community, though hard, wasn't the scariest dragon I'd faced.

The next chapter of my story began at a local adult disability centre. They were looking for musicians to volunteer every Wednesday for a music program they had just started. Music had always been incredibly important to me. I had been writing songs since the age of seven and learning the ukulele for a few months. So I decided to take the job.

After being dropped off for the first time, I walked into a school-like environment with hallways and classroom-like rooms, a staff room and a receptionist's office—everything I had learned to fear. My throat closed up, my hands began to shake and my brain turned to fog as I considered calling Mum and asking her to turn the car around and pick me up.

Too much. No thank you. Try again another day.

But whether it was my fear of other people seeing me look like a fool, or a push from God, I continued walking to the room, where I was met by my new boss. With a smile on his face and a guitar in hand, he told me what to expect, showed me the songs we'd be playing and singing, and assured me to just 'be yourself, they'll love you'—something I had never heard before.

The residents began to come in. There were people who had never spoken a day in their lives, people who had never fed themselves, people who were incontinent, people who were intellectually disabled, people who had never taken a breath on their own, people whose bodies were too weak for even a wheelchair and had arrived in mobile beds that could be tilted upwards to allow them to see, people whose vocal abilities started and finished with screaming . . . I realised that this was my first experience with disability of all aspects.

I took in a deep breath, and we started.

The playing turned into music, and that music turned into dancing. My fingers strummed at the strings of my ukulele, and I looked at this crowd of humans who were so unashamedly, wholeheartedly showing happiness and joy, completely carefree and comfortable in all that they were. Not a single person was fearful of expectation. Not one of them was hiding who they were for fear of not fitting into a false social ideology. They were simply *themselves*.

And, for the first time in my life, I understood what it meant to feel safe, to feel a sense of comfort and belonging. I hadn't realised that I had tears in my eyes, and that my strumming fingers had faltered until I felt a nudge on my shoulder. It brought me out of

And, for the first time in my life I understood what it meant to feel safe, to feel a sense of comfort and belonging.

my dream world and I saw my boss, who had a smile on his face. He nodded in the direction of the small dancing crowd, a look in his eye that I was sure meant that he had read my mind. With a smile that mirrored his, I stepped onto the floor and allowed myself to push away the social expectations that had weighed me down my entire life. I danced, and I sang. And I had people grabbing on to me, and screaming in my face, and I had never felt more at peace. I had never felt safer.

Mum had walked in some time during this mix. Later, she told me that it was the first time she had seen me like that: unaware of sensory issues, uncaring of being touched and grabbed and having loud noises in my ears, not fearful of other people in the slightest, but embracing them with everything in me. I understood these people, and they understood me. I didn't have to hide myself, or be someone I wasn't, because they didn't, either. If I got excited, if I stimmed, if I wanted to put down my ukulele and dance instead, it was okay. It was fine. It was great.

Kyeema Support Services was where I learned how to freely unmask, and freely be Chloé. It was the place where I started to unlearn my internalised ableism, unlearn the deficit framework of disability, and instead start to learn the importance of and the power in my own identity. I went to bed that night with a fire in my tummy and a passion in my heart. I was desperate for more.

Only a month later, I signed up to volunteer at the Riding for the Disabled Association (RDA). My greatest passion has always been horses. My parents told me that, even from a young age, the only time they saw me being completely *me* was around horses, and I could tell within myself that I undoubtedly belonged with them.

Horses don't judge you. They don't look at you funny when you don't understand social cues or mess up context. They don't expect anything from you, except to come as yourself. For a long time, even my horses weren't enough. But, after meeting and becoming friends with the disabled community, I knew the RDA was my next step.

Every Tuesday, I spent all day at the RDA. I caught, tacked and trained the horses before the riders arrived, and I supported and taught the riders around and on the horses. Some days, my group consisted of more advanced riders who required minimal support and I would simply help them finesse their skills and enjoy their horses. Other times, it consisted of me and a semi-verbal young boy who spoke only in *Thomas the Tank Engine* quotes and expected me to do the same—I spent a week learning every single episode by heart so I could talk with him the way that he needed me to. Or a woman who only enjoyed interacting through song and expected me to have a new Disney song learned and ready to sing every week (unflappable ponies are essential when you're giving a theatrical rendition of 'Let It Go' while you're leading them). Or a young girl who hadn't had a very good set of cards handed to her in life, whose fairytale was very much still in her Once Upon a Time and would often refuse to go near any of the adults or their horses. So, we'd sit in the paddock and talk while making daisy chains for each other.

The people who came to this group quickly became the most important people in my life. I'd be the first one there and the last one home. During lunchtime I would refuse to sit with the rest of the staff; instead, I was always eager to hang out with the riders and be surrounded by people I felt safe with. At the age of sixteen I became Australia's youngest RDA instructor. Whatever we were doing, as long as I was here, I felt like I was home.

Discovering places where you can find your tribe and, as a result, your own positive identity can be incredibly difficult. A few people might find their tribe and sanctuary without really having to look—perhaps at school, in team sports, with the people already in your life. For most of us, however, finding those places where we can unashamedly be our unmasked, full selves can be exceedingly difficult.

I had started to unearth my own sanctuaries within these communities and volunteer groups where I worked, but I was still so incredibly hurt by the outside world and tainted by the schooling system, leaving me a shell beyond these little safe spaces. I remember the day the senior RDA coach, smiling brightly and patting me on the back, told Mum when she came to pick me up that he'd never met someone who was so full of life, so positive and so eager. Mum turned to me when we got into the car and asked, 'Why are you never like that with anyone else? Why aren't you like that with me?'

Sinking into the chair, I softly answered, 'I know who I am when I'm here.'

Finding my voice

There are three things that I have always turned to whenever the world becomes too much, too scary, too intimidating: horses, fictional characters and writing.

On 11 August 2014, Robin Williams passed away. His death absolutely shattered me. As someone who struggled to find tranquillity or genuine understanding with other humans in my life, I had taken comfort in Williams. His characters showcased love, light, sadness and all the nuances of the world in the most beautiful, magical, quirky of ways, and helped me discover how to find those emotions myself.

The news of Robin's death struck me in a way that I hadn't felt before. I felt a loss of someone who seemed to know my soul.

I felt a loss of the characters that had become my best friends. In my sadness, I did what I do best. I wrote.

I sat down in my bedroom, tears flowing down my face, and poured out my heart onto the broken keys of my laptop. I was desperate to share my feelings with *someone,* to share the sadness in my heart, and to understand how sadness had permeated his being so deeply that he had taken his own life, despite the happiness he had given to those around him.

Here is what I wrote that day:

Robin Williams died today.
Here is a list of things that Robin Williams was:

funny
sharp
kind
clever
and sad.

That's important, the 'and sad', because sometimes sadness can feel like the only thing we are. It can feel all-encompassing. It can feel like the only thing anyone could possibly see when they look at you: sad. That person is so, so, sad.

But there is always an 'and'. We are never just sad. We are never only. We are always and.

We have all known people who were sad, who are sad; some of us are ourselves sad. Being sad does not remove the other parts of us, though it can make them harder for us to see. When you are sad, you don't necessarily feel like you are also funny, and sharp, and clever, and kind.

But you still are. You don't have to feel like something to be it.

Those things are written on your bones, they are woven into the fabric of your skin. Sadness can feel so big, so big and overwhelming and complete, even when it is not a directed sadness. Maybe especially when it is not a directed sadness, when it's a depression that has no direct cause and nothing we can name.

Sometimes the sadness is too big. People try to cut it out, or starve it out, or drink it down, or drug it silent. If this is you: I'm sorry. If this is you: you are not alone. If this is you: remember that the solution is never to give up, because you do not live in a vacuum. There are people waiting for you. There are films and songs and books and not-sadness waiting for you. I know that you don't feel like waiting, but wait anyway.

If you need help, ask for it.

Robin Williams died today, but the Genie didn't, and Mrs Doubtfire didn't, and Peter Pan didn't. Sean Maguire didn't, and Professor Philip Brainard didn't, and Alan Parrish didn't. Batty Koda didn't. John Keating didn't. You didn't.

Don't.

And then I hit 'Post'.

I'm still not sure what it was that nudged me into making this diary entry viewable to the public eye. Perhaps I was desperate for others to feel as deeply as I did. Perhaps this was my first real understanding of the sadness of the world from another person's perspective, and I was desperate to change it. But, as I pressed the deep blue 'Post' button on Facebook and sent off my feelings into cyberspace, I realised it was one of the first times in my life that I had allowed myself to feel and experience emotion on a public level. It was the first time I had been able to identify and put my emotions in an internal folder, instead of falling into a fiery pit of confusion and uncertainty.

I expected that my post would remain with my thirty-odd Facebook friends—mainly Irish family members I hadn't seen since I was a child, and the one or two peers I had met at the pony club or theatre. But, within a couple days, it had clocked up over one hundred shares—a large and terrifying number for a seventeen year old who refused to attend our local farmers' market for fear of crowds.

One of those shares was from a psychologist friend of Mum's, who asked if I would mind if she shared my entry on her website. It was something that seemed both confusing and worrying to me. *What if people laughed? What if people teased? What if it sparked something? What if it didn't?*

My emotions have always been important and private to me. I have always felt on a deep level, so allowing those emotions to become public stirred a whole new array of uncertainty and feelings. But cautiously, I agreed, and my post about sadness quickly gained traction.

From the safety of a pink-cased One Direction-stickered computer I watched as views and comments flooded onto my Facebook page.

> *'This is the first time I've seen life explained like this.'*
> *'I'm going to start focusing on the "ands" of my life.'*
> *'Please. Write more.'*

These comments from people who didn't know me, and who I didn't know, remarking on how they identified with my post, made me realise that my writing had ignited something in them. I experienced a sense of solidarity with a world I had felt alienated from. I had seen a sparkle—and I desperately wanted more.

Writing had always been one of my outlets but, until that post, it had been contained in an orange *The Saddle Club* journal and the back pages of my math book. There I would write stories of far-off worlds and anthropomorphised animals—metaphors for human rights issues, my own feelings of powerlessness, the intense feelings I had, but could not show. But now I felt these stories could be heard.

If I could write about sadness, maybe I could write something else, too. Maybe there was a way for me to find more of that sparkle that had lit up a previously dull world.

Once again, I sat down at my laptop with its peeling-off 'Future Mrs Tomlinson' and 'One Band, One Dream, One Direction' stickers. This time I decided to write about something else that was incredibly important to me, something that had shaped my entire life to this point and would continue to do so. Something that was a crucial part of my identity, but still felt so alien, so *not me.* It was one of the most terrifying things that I could possibly think of to write about publicly: being autistic.

Despite having had the diagnosis for a few years by now, I still felt little comfort in it. People were not speaking to me anymore because of it, it had sparked more online bullying despite my not attending school anymore, and I had found few resources other than fearmongering articles by so-called professionals. These 'expert' articles were the last thing in the world I wanted to read, or hear about, or envision my mind to be. They were terrifying, and they left me with feelings of loneliness and isolation that remained as intense as they had before my diagnosis. So, I did what any typical Gen Z would do in my situation. I took to the internet, writing out my deepest, darkest feelings in the form of an anonymous blog, written under the pseudonym 'Princess Aspien'.

I called it *God Help the Outcasts*, and I shared my story to the world in the form of Disney metaphors, poems and honest thoughts that I had bottled up for far too long. The post started with:

When I was younger, I always felt like an outcast. While I didn't have a hunchback or a disfigured face like Quasimodo, I could relate to how he felt rejected by society.

And it finished with:

And now here I am at the age of seventeen. I'm still the same frizzy haired, green-eyed girl who would rather chat aimlessly to one of my four cats than any human, refuses to eat with a proper spoon, can't eat red food, and breaks into Disney musicals in the middle of Safeway. But I'm not worried about it anymore. Because this is who I am, and this is who I'm meant to be.

I didn't fully believe what I was writing at this stage, but I desperately wanted to. My sole intention of the blog was to scream out to the universe. Through his characters, which all showcased the importance of friendship and identity in the most beautiful of ways, Mr Robin Williams had taught me that finding your sidekick is one of the greatest things you can do, and I was so desperate to find that person, those people.

I was a trapped genie, desperate to escape from my prison.

I was praying, waiting, hoping for someone else who was like me, and for the first time I was shouting my truest mind, my deepest feelings into the abyss instead of swallowing them or filing them away. What I didn't expect was for the abyss to speak back. But I suppose Genie never expected to find Aladdin, who would free him.

Almost overnight, my little anonymous blog began getting thousands of views due to this wonderful thing called 'share to Facebook' and a small number of autistic people, parents and 'mum groups' who had begun to share it far and wide. As the number of views rose, so did the number of comments from people around the globe who had shared my exact experiences.

'Finally! Someone just like me!'
'You've just made me realise that I'm not alone.'
'This is the first time that I've ever read something that I relate to.'

I felt seen. Maybe this crash-landed rocket ship wasn't a solo mission, after all. Maybe fairytales were for everyone, including me.

That blog quickly became the most important thing in the world to me. Every time I felt lonely, or lost, or confused, or like my home planet was too far away, I would sit down and write from the deepest parts of my heart. I shared the hardest parts of my life. I shared the best days of my life. I turned my blog into my online journal, and I felt a sense of safety and community in comments from others who obviously felt like they came from the same planet as me.

I had found a place where I wasn't different, or strange, or unusual. I was just Chloé—or, to my readers, Princess Aspien—and all the parts of me were exactly as they should be.

Let it go

My next feet-finding experience with stepping out and beginning to embrace the world came in the form of a Princess Anna costume that I got for my seventeenth birthday. At this point in my life, Disney's *Frozen* was my hyper-fixation. I had found immediate comfort in Anna's character and her bold, bubbly, unapologetic personality—the sort of person I aspired to be, and that I knew I could be when I was volunteering in the disability centre or with my horses. But I also knew I had the potential to be like that always, if only ostracism and negative opinions hadn't hung over me like a rain cloud.

The moment I decked myself out in the four-layered, six-piece dress, brunette pigtailed wig, pink cape and black boots with pink designs painted across them, I was no longer *Chloé: fearful of the world, shy and quiet*. I no longer felt the weight of society's unwritten and unnecessary expectations. Instead, I was simply Anna.

Growing up in a world that is so clearly not designed for us, and where the traits that we naturally feel and portray are deemed to be odd, strange and unwanted, it's extremely difficult for neurodivergent people to find a 'real life' person to relate to. It's part of the reason why I so deeply adored working at the disability centre—we had all been through similar experiences, and we were each other's only true 'real life' sanctuary.

Instead of finding friendship with other people, many of us end up finding that connection, that validation, those 'they're like me' moments through our favourite fantasy characters, or even public figures, whether YouTubers, actors or singers. These characters offer us refuge, and a way to learn social skills. Some of the most exciting moments of my life have been when I was compared to the YouTuber Grav3yardgirl and Princess Anna, both of whom I was obsessed with and had based my personality upon at the time the comparisons were made. Both of these figures gave me lifelong social skills that I use to this day.

Dressing as Anna, I discovered that I was able to take on her personality traits, her zest, her love for life, her confidence, her complete 'I am who I am' attitude, and it was intoxicating. I finally felt like *me* when I was dressed up as a princess from an animated children's film. On multiple occasions, seventeen-year-old me begged Mum to allow me to dress up as Anna when we were going shopping, or to the movies, or to pick up my siblings from school—she ever so gently suggested that it might be a better idea to just leave the costume at home.

A few months after my seventeenth birthday, my dream of going public as Princess Anna came true, when my boss at the Kyeema centre, who was friends with me on Facebook, saw one of my many posts in which I was dressed as her and asked if I would come and dress up for the residents. In another setting, a suggestion like this would have resulted in an immediate and firm 'absolutely not'—or, more likely, me quietly telling Mum my answer, so she could tell them for me. But I had a safe refuge at Kyeema. I had been volunteering at the centre two days a week for some time, and it had well and truly become my second home. So, I eagerly agreed.

That performance turned into another, which turned into another, which turned into my confidence in my identity growing, which turned into being asked to perform at the local fair, which turned into me not even caring when some of my bullies turned up at the fair and recognised me. The fair gig turned into more performances, which turned into me being asked to do children's birthday parties, parades and charities, which turned into me owning and running my very own award-winning character and entertainment company complete with twelve characters before I was eighteen.

It was during this time, with my confidence growing stronger than it ever had before, that I came to a realisation: *If I can be this person that I have always dreamed of being when I am dressed as a princess, there is no reason why I can't also be that person when I am dressed as just Chloé.*

Isn't it ironic, that because of a fictional, fairytale character, I was able to learn how to be completely, indisputably myself? How sad, that the only place I *could* find myself was in a fictional, fairytale character.

Although a long time coming, and in a somewhat unusual way (though, what else can you expect from me?), that realisation kick-started my journey into being the person I am today. A person who is boldly me, a person who is proudly me.

It shouldn't have taken me as long as it did to find the resources and community that I needed to discover this person. The lack of genuine, helpful resources created both for and by disabled people is a large reason why it took such an unnecessary amount of time, along with a deficit framework of thinking and a refusal to give those of us who don't fit societal standards a chance.

It is vital that we build and maintain communities that are accessible, attainable and available to all. It is vital that those who have not been given an opportunity to truly discover their identities, due to no fault of their own, find the same feeling of identity and sense of belonging as everyone else.

I'm still discovering my identity each and every day. Every single day, I find out something new about Chloé Hayden. I learn a little bit more about the person I was, the person I am, and the person that I'm becoming. And that's okay. I don't think we need to be in a rush to discover everything straight away.

As Robin Williams in the role of Teddy Roosevelt in *Night at the Museum* so beautifully put it, 'It's time for your next adventure'. He smiles as Larry, the hero of the film, exhales a breath and tells him, 'I have no idea what I'm going to do tomorrow'. To which Teddy, in all his wisdom, responds, 'How exciting'.

Your life is exciting. Discovering your identity is exciting. And you should be in no rush to figure out this huge puzzle all at once; there's no time limit, no award for the first and the fastest. Take the time you need to discover and accept who you are, to discover what your story is. You're allowed to rewrite chapters, you're allowed to get writer's block, you're allowed to change the genre.

Give yourself the freedom to explore, to learn, to simply be in your own time, at your own pace. You deserve and need the time and the space and the opportunity to freely, openly, safely, wholeheartedly discover who you are and who you're supposed to be, free from fear, free from accusation, free from expectation.

HOW TO FIND COMFORT IN WHO YOU ARE

Discovering who we are is just one part of our fairytale ... But learning to find comfort in that identity is a whole new chapter. Here are some ways that you can learn to find comfort in all that you are.

Read, watch and learn from others

Textbooks written by psychologists are fine, but *real* research and understanding comes from the community itself. Follow YouTubers who are autistic/queer/disabled/POC/whatever it may be. Read blogs and books written by people in the community. Fill your Instagram feed and For You page with positive voices.

Find support and friendship groups

Joining up with my local autism group was such an instrumental step in accepting my identity as an autistic person. Being surrounded by people I knew were just like me, where I didn't have to hide or pretend, was huge in being able to open up and accept myself. I was also able to find friendships at a time when finding people who truly loved me for me was incredibly difficult.

Get involved

I learned about the community, about others and about myself through local disability advocacy groups. It is such an empowering part of my fairytale. Get involved in your local groups, conferences, volunteer organisations and youth groups. You never know, you may be the voice that someone has been waiting for.

Surround yourself with love

If someone doesn't accept you in all that you are . . . get rid of them! You do *not* deserve to go through life weighed down by people who do not care, love, accept and embrace your authentic self. Your people are out there. Surround yourself with those who give you love and understanding. People who don't see you for you do not deserve to be written into your fairytale. You are the author of your story. Don't let other people take your pen.

Start your own blog

At a time when I was so sure there was no one else like me on the planet, creating a blog was where I found my people and felt like my voice could finally be heard. Start a blog, create a TikTok clip, write a book . . . there are people who will want to listen to you and perhaps also want to share their stories, too.

CHAPTER 8

Eye Sparkles

Among my most favourite moments in all Disney movies is just after the climax scene, when an absolute banger of a tune by Hans Zimmer or Elton John or Phil Collins or Alan Menken is played behind scenes that are cinematic masterpieces, such as Simba heroically deciding to go back to Pride Rock to take his rightful place as the King of Africa, or Kenai in *Brother Bear* discovering who he truly is as the spirits of his ancestors transform him into a bear, or Aladdin finding his true love and Genie becoming free. Or even better, the ending scene in *Mr. Magorium's Wonder Emporium* when, after years of doubting herself and not knowing what her sparkle is, Molly Mahoney, in all of her glory, discovers it.

Those moments so wonderfully showcase what it's like for all of us when we have our 'sparkle' moments—when we realise who we truly are and unlock the powers that were inside of us all along. But it's never without a journey beforehand; it's never without the battle scenes, and the dragon slaying, and the sword fights.

These moments reveal what I call our 'eye sparkles', those things that ignite a passion in us so deeply that it fills our every crevice.

Our eye sparkles are there from the beginning, and I believe with every part of my being that they're the most exquisite parts of us, but it often takes those climactic moments for us to see and appreciate them.

Discovering eye sparkles

After my initial blog post blew up and started circling the interwebs, I started to rediscover my passion for writing. I wrote blog posts almost daily, sharing stories of myself, sharing posts about autism, sharing about my life and the way I saw the world. I suppose at the time I saw it like an online diary for an audience of real people, rather than writing to the abyss. What I didn't expect, however, was for these people to write back to me. What I didn't expect was to see myself in every single person who posted their story in the comments.

People began reciprocating by sharing their stories, their fairytales, their experiences. I heard from people all over the world, from all walks of life, of all genders and all ages, and I started to discover something in these people. Not only did they all have stories similar to mine, fairytales that were written in the same style as my own, but there was something else. Every single one of them included a feature that to them likely seemed unimportant and unremarkable, but that I immediately recognised as the most important, magical feature a person can possess: an eye sparkle.

Eye sparkles. Superpowers. Gifts. Adorations. These are things that make people tick, that give them a zest for life, that make them feel powerful, excited, happy. Something that is completely, utterly marvellous to them. In autism these are called 'special interests' or, in ADHD terminology, 'hyper-fixations'. We see them as quirks, obsessions, something odd and curious and not of the norm.

Those special interests in autism are often, stereotypically, trains, gadgets or science. In autistic women, they may lean more towards bands, books and films. Frequently these special interests or hyper-fixations are quickly judged as harmful; schools, autism groups and therapy centres may even attempt to limit them or make them accessible only as a form of so-called 'positive reinforcement'. But these special interests, these quirks, these obsessions are so much more.

In *Mr. Magorium's Wonder Emporium* (the best film ever created—no, I will not be taking constructive criticism of that), we meet Molly Mahoney, a finger-drumming childhood prodigy pianist who can't quite tap into her potential and is stuck on how to finish her first piano composition. Those who love her can see her sparkle, although she can't seem to figure it out herself. We follow Molly as she desperately tries to fit into who she believes she's supposed to be and what she believes she's supposed to do, while working at a magical toy store on the side.

Molly is a beautiful oddball of a human, as is the owner of the toy store, an eccentric 243-year-old inventor who has probably survived so long due to his incapacity to become bored. Her two other sidekicks come in the form of a ten-year-old boy with an extravagant hat collection and an inability to make friends his own age, and an accountant lovingly nicknamed 'The Mutant', who is so holed up in his work and image that 'fun' is not in his vocabulary.

Perhaps the reason why this movie became one of my biggest fixations to date (for five years, I watched it twice a day every single day—I'm happy to announce I have since pulled this back to once every two weeks) is due to all four protagonists being so very clearly coded as autistic. But perhaps another reason why I still find so much comfort, love and understanding in this film is that it so beautifully showcases eye sparkles. And when we allow ourselves to wholeheartedly be our wonderful, quirky selves, those sparkles can finally show themselves in all of their glory.

At the end of the film, Molly not only composes 'Molly Mahoney's First', but also finds the magic within herself. It is her magic, her eye sparkle, her finger-tapping stimming and new-found self-understanding that leads her to both compose her musical piece and save the toy store. (I'm rambling, I know. But in my defence, this *is* my book. I cannot be expected to not word-vomit about *Mr. Magorium's Wonder Emporium* at least once.) Despite this film being geared towards children, it's one we can all use to better understand our own eye sparkles, and the important place that they have in us, and the world around us.

Once upon a time, experts believed that special interests were an avoidance activity, something that autistic people would do to manage negative and big emotions, such as anxiety. They were called 'obsessions', and autistic people with intense special interests (about 95 per cent of the autistic population) were called inflexible, rigid and stubborn. Special interests were taken away, or used as a reward for good behaviour, and were often seen as causing autistic people to regress, become incapable of accomplishing tasks, or avoid social interaction. Special interests were seen as negative—and still are in many forms of Applied Behaviour Analysis (ABA)-style therapy, where they are used as bribery and rewards for good behaviour and are removed when a child is not behaving as is deemed socially appropriate.

But research and scientists have finally started to catch up with what autistic people have been saying for decades: special interests are not a burden; they are not a hindrance. Special interests, eye sparkles, can drastically improve a person's life in so many ways. They are so much more than odd little quirks and seemingly unnecessary fixations. They're a crucial, vital part of a person's life, especially in childhood.

My eye sparkles

Growing up, I had a new eye sparkle just about every week (the fact that I wasn't diagnosed with ADHD until I was twenty-two absolutely astounds me), but some of my biggest eye sparkles were (and still are) animals, the *Titanic* and performing—all eye sparkles that have benefitted me throughout my life.

When I was four, I got stung by a fire ant on my grandparents' farm. My grandmother saw the ant on me and, well aware of their painful, potentially dangerous sting, began to panic. I watched as Nanny hurried over to the phone to call my grandfather, Kenpa, who's a doctor, in order to work out what we needed to do, and how intensely we needed to panic about this supposedly vicious bite. In all of my young wisdom, I brushed the ant off, and calmly walked over to tell Nanny that she need not worry, as I was bitten by a boy ant, not a girl ant, and boy ants can't *actually* sting you and, therefore, there was no need to panic.

When I was five, I began horse-riding lessons after begging my parents for them since I was two. My parents tell me that the moment I saw a horse there was a physical change in me—every worry and fear bottled up inside my little body disappeared, replaced with calm and happiness. When I was with horses, nothing else in the whole world mattered. I began weekly riding lessons, my parents driving a two-hour round trip every single Saturday just so I could have my one hour of pure bliss and peace.

When I was ten, and my struggles were at an all-time high, we moved to a property in rural Victoria where I could have my own horses and be surrounded by them constantly. Without a doubt, I know that move saved my life. Horses were my first, and still to this day my greatest, eye sparkle. At the age of twenty-two, after several state and national titles, I travelled to Texas by myself to compete in the Extreme Cowboy World Finals—I placed eleventh in the world on a horse that I had been training for four weeks, while many other competitors had had their horses for a decade.

For my ninth birthday, we went to a pop-up *Titanic* exhibition at a museum and I was awestruck. An entire exhibit with multiple rooms and hundreds of artefacts about the liner. I was in absolute paradise until . . . I noticed that one of the 1317 names on the passenger board was wrong. I'd like to remind you that at this time of my life I was selectively mute, had intense social anxiety, and didn't speak to anyone except for my family. However, there was something *wrong*. The passenger's name was *wrong*. It was unjust, it was *unacceptable*.

Imagine a nine-year-old girl dressed in a sparkly purple dress, pink Barbie shoes and her hair in two plaits, with a look of pure and utter determination as she let go of Kenpa's hand in order to storm over to the service counter, where a young museum worker quickly discovered the wrath of an undiagnosed autistic child whose special interest had been compromised. My intense feelings of justice would not settle until the matter was handled correctly. I told her very firmly (or, as firmly as a nine year old could manage) that their exhibit was wrong and that for the sake of the passenger's honour, it needed to be changed. *Immediately*. I proceeded to tell her and other staff about various facts from the exhibit that were missing or outdated, and that it wasn't up to par, and that I would be more than happy to provide them with the correct information so the exhibit could be accurate, instead of a work of fiction.

Why I didn't get dragged out of that exhibit by my ears remains a mystery.

A couple weeks later, we received an email from the museum, announcing that they had done further research and realised their mistakes. They were changing the incorrect information and offered us free tickets to the updated exhibit.

At the age of fifteen, I nearly got evicted from another museum for insisting to a tour guide that the *Titanic* had only three funnels. The fourth was only for decoration and was used for ventilation (a fact of common knowledge, I would have thought. *Truly, come on now*!).

Growing up, I desperately wanted to be a performer. I wanted to be a singer, a dancer, an actor. I was also selectively mute and entirely uncoordinated. Mum (who was an actor) used to joke that the only way I could be one was if I was a French mime. Dad would say that I couldn't even walk in a straight line. Both had valid points and, yet, the two of them did everything in their power to get me into every performance class within an hour's drive so I could sing, dance and act to my heart's content.

I was beyond horrid. I actually ended up getting kicked out of several dance schools because I was deemed unteachable, and my Year 5 music teacher hit me and told me her infant son would have been a better choice to lead the school musical. But I was in my element. And never once did my parents tell me that I couldn't do something. Never once did they sneeze at the idea of a selectively mute, chronically uncoordinated young girl becoming a famous performer. My passions, no matter how bizarre and unlikely, were never once teased or dismissed by those who loved me. Instead, they told me to reach for my dreams.

As it turned out, acting and performing didn't just give me a way to find my voice. They ended up being my entire career.

At the age of twenty-three, on the night of 26 March 2021, while visiting a tiny town on the border of Victoria and New South Wales, I got a call from my acting agent that would change my life. For the past few months, I had been auditioning for a little show called *Heartbreak High*. I had received dozens of callbacks and attended a number of rehearsals and meetings. But after so many of these, I had presumed this latest one would be unsuccessful. But, at 9.30 pm, having just stepped off the stage after giving a talk, I answered the phone to hear my agent say, 'I have some good news. Are you sitting down?'

Because my loved ones and I had embraced my eye sparkle of performing, it grew into a lead role in a Netflix series, where I was not only one of three leads, but also the first autistic actress to be cast in an Australian television show, and the second autistic person in the world to play an autistic character.

I found my confidence when I was performing, when I was horse riding, when I was lecturing fully grown adults on the *Titanic*. When I was engaging in my special interests, I wasn't scared, I wasn't timid, I wasn't mute. My eye sparkles inspired me to create the life, and the person I am now.

Our eye sparkles make us stronger

Eye sparkles, superpowers, special interests, whatever they may be are vital to the growth of neurodivergent kids. They are something we need to focus on, celebrate and encourage.

There is such a huge push in our world towards finding interests in the common, in the practical—sports, popular culture, math—but when a person's focus is on something that isn't considered 'normal', it's condemned, pushed away and worried over. This is seen often in the way teenagers interact on social media and at school. The idea behind 'cringe culture' (cyberbullying of people who appear socially unacceptable and different, whether due to interests, appearance or habits) is deeply rooted in ableism, and directly affects autistic people and anyone else who does not conform.

Neurotypical society has repeatedly ostracised, excluded and abused autistic and otherwise disabled and neurodivergent people out of dominant social groups, leaving many of us to find sanctuary and friendship in places that may be deemed 'uncool' (truly, a ridiculous word in the first place—who decides whether something is or is not cool?). We find safety in online fandoms, in groups and clubs, in places where 'everyone else is a weirdo', and that's okay. Common neurodivergent special interests are often seen as uncool, unpopular, socially unacceptable. But, then, neurotypical people will sometimes discover them and co-opt those groups and interests, leaving us to once again be the targets of bullying and harassment.

A few years ago, fidget spinners and weighted blankets, which were created for neurodivergent people, became a popular craze everywhere and were seen as cool. Ironic, given that those who used them previously were ostracised for having them as support needs. And then, this craze died out as quickly as it began, leaving neurodivergent people who still need them to once again be seen as 'uncool', as 'weird'. If you bully people for using fidget toys, for enjoying certain shows or being a part of certain fandoms, if you tease 'band kids' or 'theatre nerds' or 'horse girls' or 'anime kids' or whatever other thing we have decided to create a trope of, if you snicker at people who dress differently to you, who move differently to you, who look different than you, you are partaking in cringe culture, and you are directly participating in ableism.

The world is constantly telling us to hide the parts of ourselves that are not considered perfectly normal . . . It's ruining us all.

During school, I struggled immensely with math. I spent every single class hunched over my book crying because the equations looked like a toddler's scribbles and the teacher may as well have been speaking Latin (a language that, if the analogy was not clear enough, I do not speak). Even now, I can barely do basic mathematics. My eight-year-old sister will show me her math homework and it still looks like another language to me.

I was also banned from food tech in school because I set the microwave on fire. Twice. I gave some kid quite severe food poisoning as well. I can't read an analogue clock, I can't drive a car, I struggle to cook, I can't eat red food. Some days, I struggle to look after myself. I still need to be reminded to eat, and drink, and go to the toilet, and brush my hair. Some days, simply talking is too much. There are so many things that people half my age have been doing for years now (except for perhaps the 'drive a car' bit), and there are things that I know I will struggle with and need extra support with for the rest of my life. But, there are things that I can do better than just about anyone.

I'm an incredible public speaker, and actor. I learned that from my special interest in Princess Anna. I have a huge heart for social justice, and will never back down when human, animal or environmental rights are under attack or when I know something is wrong—even if it may get me in trouble. I learned that from the *Titanic* exhibition at the museum. I can walk into any room and make it mine. I can talk to anyone in the world, I can now make friends with anyone. I learned that from volunteering with community groups. I can ride any horse, and will take on, rescue and understand any animal—mammal, fish, reptile, bird or amphibian. I learned that from those animal encyclopaedias that I read religiously, and my lifelong connection with horses, because animals have always understood me better than any human.

My eye sparkles have given me my career, my life, my personality. They made me who I am. Screw normality. I don't need math or school food tech or perfect executive functioning to succeed in the way that Chloé Hayden's story is written.

My talents, the things I love, my eye sparkles, those are the most important parts of me. They're the most important parts of all of us. We need to stop focusing on the things we can't do or struggle with—this is especially so for neurodivergent people—and focus instead on what our eye sparkles are. If we only focus on what we can't do, if we only focus on the bad, if we only focus on our struggles, we will never find our Happily Ever After. We will continuously be wading through mud, creeping through an elephant graveyard, stuck like Genie in a lamp.

If we only focus on what we can't do, if we only focus on the bad, if we only focus on our struggles, we will never find our Happily Ever After.

In *The Lion King*, Pumbaa says, 'We have to put our past behind us' and Rafiki reminds us, 'Remember who we are'.

If Simba had only looked at the bad side of different, he never would have become king.

Genie and Quasimodo would have never become free.

I wouldn't be sitting here today, writing this book, living my dreams.

I decided to focus on my eye sparkles, instead of the things that I couldn't do. I decided to focus on me, to focus on the most beautiful parts of me. I've been able to see what my Happily Ever After is going to be, not in spite of my differences, but because of my eye sparkles.

WHY YOU NEED TO FIND YOUR EYE SPARKLE

Our special interests are so much more than a quirky obsession, or a fun hobby. They're fundamental parts of our being that have the ability to drastically, positively alter our lives when we nurture, respect and foster them. Here are just a few things eye sparkles can do for you.

Open career paths

Many neurodivergent people get into and thrive in lines of work that accommodate their special interests. Chances are, you are going to flourish in something that you adore.

Lead to friendships

With neurodivergent children often struggling to make friends in typical situations, getting involved in groups, clubs and activities that cater their interest is a brilliant way to build both friendships and social skills.

Reduce stress

When you are engaging in your special interest, it releases dopamine and this can ground and relax you.

Build life skills

Engaging and learning about special interests can drastically increase life skills—not necessarily just in the interest-specific sector, but also socially.

HOW TO DISCOVER YOUR EYE SPARKLES

Our eye sparkles are ingrained into us—they're a part of our very being, and often you'll know from a young age exactly what this eye sparkle is. Sometimes, though, these eye sparkles might take a bit of extra effort to discover.

Ask the people around you

Sometimes it can be difficult to find our own eye sparkles, especially in a world where our talents, loves and interests are often ridiculed or dismissed, leaving us to bury them, or belittle their importance and brilliance. Ask the people around you what they think your eye sparkles are. I guarantee they'll have answers. They may know you better than you know yourself.

Try things out

Join community groups, check out your school clubs, find online tutorials. Allow yourself to try things out and see what sticks. You may discover a love, a talent, a joy that you didn't expect.

Go easy on yourself

It took Beethoven years to write many of his symphonies. It took Leonardo da Vinci years to paint the *Mona Lisa*. Notre Dame took 180 years to build. Your eye sparkle does not have to become your greatest asset overnight . . . or, even at all. Take your time, go easy on yourself. Find love in things simply to be in love with them.

What do you love?

Your eye sparkle doesn't have to mean playing Mozart by the time you're four, or having a superhuman knowledge of every chemical, or creating paintings that would put Picasso to shame. What do you *love* doing? What do you *love* reading about? What makes *your* heart sing? What could you talk about for hours on end and never grow tired of doing so?

Perhaps you love making LEGO, or building worlds on Minecraft, or reading every book, sequel and fanfiction of a particular series. Maybe you adore animals, or cars, or creative writing. Your loves don't have to be groundbreaking to be magical.

Whatever makes your heart sing is the greatest eye sparkle in the world.

CHAPTER 9

Adulting

The mere notion of being an 'adult' once brought me complete and utter fear. Any variation of or association with that word—grown-up, older, birthday and so on—would make my heart race like Vanellope von Schweetz in her candy racing cart. It would turn my mind as dark and fearful as the elephant graveyard. Even before I understood the concept of growing up, before I really knew what it meant, I was petrified of it.

The first time I specifically remember being hit with the 'I don't want to grow up' bug was the night before my seventh birthday. An overwhelming feeling of doom, fear and panic cascaded through my body, and I tiptoed, trembling, into Mum and Dad's bedroom, slipped under the covers and proceeded to sob my still six-year-old heart out, begging them to fix me, begging for a remedy. Wasn't there some sort of injection that would keep me a six year old forever? (An incredibly large offer on my part, as injections had long been my biggest fear. Or second biggest, I suppose, because I would have taken a million of those little suckers if it meant not having to face growing up.)

There are a lot of reasons why growing up has always been so scary to me: the idea of change, of leaving things behind, of being 'unable' to do the kid stuff that I love doing, of expectations that I won't be able to meet. Significant occasions and milestones, such as birthdays and graduations—occasions most young people see as monumental and thrilling—scared the living bejeezus out of me as it meant becoming closer to adulthood, something I well and truly did *not* want to be a part of. They guaranteed change and marked the end of a time that can never be brought back.

I suppose that's the thing with life, and with growing up. It's always change, it's always new, it's always different. While changes and new things and differences still absolutely terrify me, I've now come to understand them. So, allow me to take you on a little tour of adulthood, of the different, new world it creates—told through the eyes of a girl who absolutely, completely, adamantly did not want to grow up.

Periods

I cried when I got my period (and let's be honest, that's reasonable).

Periods were always an open topic of conversation in my household. They were never seen as taboo, to be discussed in whispers or embarrassed about. Still, I didn't want anything to do with them. The day I got my period when I was thirteen, my mum threw a party. A literal party in which there was cake and ice cream and chocolate and balloons and presents, including a beautiful gold bracelet with 'beautiful woman' engraved on it.

Despite the celebration, I was once more reduced to tears, begging for some form of vaccine to stop me from growing up. This new chapter of my life signified so much more than just 'my first period'. It meant immense changes, it meant being a woman, it meant everything I thought I knew about myself was gone, it meant learning new things about myself. It. Sucked.

Periods can be a great challenge for autistic folk. Studies have now shown that autistic people who menstruate have higher rates of menstrual problems, including irregular cycles, unusually painful periods and excessive bleeding. Polycystic ovarian syndrome is 2.5 times more frequent, early onset puberty seven times more frequent and hormone-based acne four times more frequent for autistic folk. Those with epilepsy have their seizure activity exacerbated by hormonal changes during menstruation.

On top of these physical reactions, our sensory issues are heightened during menstruation, making it all the more overwhelming and uncomfortable. As an autistic person, I'm hyper aware of my body and all the things that are consistently happening to it. I grow frustrated because my heartbeat feels too hard, or my eyelashes are too loud when I blink, or I can smell the fabric softener on my clothes from three washes ago. So, when you're on your period and your senses are heightened, it's utterly overload central.

Sensory issues are going to happen—welcome to the wonderful world of being autistic—but there are things that you can do to manage them during your period, and to make sure you look after yourself.

HOW TO COPE WITH YOUR PERIOD

Preparation is key! Preparing for my period means being sure I always have my period products with me so I'm ready and, even when it comes at a time that isn't entirely convenient, I can still do what I can to make it manageable.

Track your cycle

Tracking your cycle, so you can be prepared a few days before your period arrives, is hugely beneficial. One of the best ways I've found to do this is through an app that allows me to put in the start and finish dates of previous periods; it then calculates when the next one is likely to arrive. It takes the surprise out the equation—most of the time. If your periods tend to be irregular, it can be a bit more difficult. By tracking my period, I'm able to make sure I'm wearing my period undies a couple of days beforehand so I don't face any spills or leaks, and I can check my calendar to make sure I'm not doing anything unnecessarily big during the worst few days.

Alternatively, simply reading the signs your body gives you is incredibly helpful, especially if your periods are irregular. I know that about three days before my period begins I will get cramps and sore boobs, and I feel lethargic and just not myself. Ding! Ding! Ding! Congratulations, it's your period. Learning your body's signs means you can be all set for when it arrives.

Choose your products

Figure out which product works best for you. I tried every product under the sun and found issues with absolutely all of them—pads were uncomfortable and leaked after an hour, tampons were scary and uncomfortable, and so on. Available products include:

★ sanitary pads (disposable or reusable)
★ menstrual cups
★ menstrual discs
★ tampons
★ period underwear.

Personally, I'm a passionate advocate of period undies. They're the only thing I've found that doesn't cause me further discomfort, and I can wear them throughout the whole month. Whatever works for you is what's of utmost importance here.

It's also important to understand that while there's a huge push at the moment for environmental sustainability (which is amazing!), this isn't always going to be possible, or the most comfortable option for you. If single-use products such as disposable pads or tampons are what's best for you, then that's what's best for you. Don't compromise your health and wellbeing—there are plenty of other opportunities to make choices for environmental reasons, and this doesn't have to be one of them. No guilt.

Make self-care a priority

Poor executive functioning and burnout caused by sensory overload can make periods difficult. Caring for your hygiene, changing products and basic self-care can feel overwhelming, or can go completely out the window. To help you manage, try:

- ★ setting an app or alarm to remind yourself to change your products
- ★ choosing a product that can be used for a little bit longer without complications, such as period undies, which don't have to be changed throughout the day. Products such as tampons need to be changed regularly and failing to do so can lead to infections such as toxic shock syndrome.

Usually, I'll do what I can to be in my own environment during my period, when my sensory levels go through the roof. Being in a place that I know and feel safe in is the best option for me. Emotionally, I make sure I'm gentle with myself—something often easier said than done. There's such a sense in our society that when it comes to periods, we must simply suck it up, despite many experiencing cramps that are worse than appendicitis pain. And it can be easy to allow these false ideas to permeate our thinking. I can't remember how many times I have passed out, or vomited for hours, or been physically unable to move—forcing myself to continue working by telling myself, *It's fine. It's just your period. Half the population gets it. Get over yourself.* Our uteruses are shedding, our hip bones are literally expanding, our muscles are contracting. We're allowed to rest, dammit.

This need for rest can be difficult for some people to understand. If you were born AMAB (assigned male at birth), your body runs on a 24-hour cycle, with your testosterone levels being highest in the morning. This means you are at your most productive then and, gradually, your hormone levels lower throughout the day, so in the evening your body is winding down. Typically, your body runs exactly as the clock does, and your energy, hormone levels and rest cycles will coincide almost perfectly with it. However, if you were born AFAB (assigned female at birth), your body works on a twenty-eight-day cycle, meaning there will be whole days where your hormone levels are at their lowest, with your body needing to rest and recover, the same way someone who's AMAB will feel at night. AFAB bodies are designed to need days of rest, so stop trying to push yourself to benefit a male- and capitalist-centric society.

Being kind to myself during my period means not pushing myself, being gentle with myself when I can't work and allowing myself to take down days. The world is not going to end because I chose to spend a day watching movies and drinking tea with a heat pack. Making sure I validate what I need during my period, and not tossing away those needs because of what either I or society expects from me, is the most important thing in the world.

WHEN BEST-LAID PLANS FAIL

Periods like to show themselves at the most inconvenient of times. One time I was travelling on my own, flying to England to see Louis Tomlinson in concert after he had announced that he wouldn't be touring Australia that year. (So, as any sane human would, I made it my mission to fly across the world to see him.) Despite having planned everything to a T and working out that my period was still two weeks away—giving me more than enough time to travel—my period decided to make herself known early. Due to my apparent perfect scheduling, I had absolutely no products with me. My painfully shy, socially anxious self nearly had an aneurysm coughing up the confidence to ask a flight attendant if there were any products available.

After a 'no', and a 'don't worry, I'll go have a look, though', I was absolutely mortified to hear her announce very clearly over the plane's loudspeaker that the young lady with the Harry Styles jumper in seat 3A needed period products.

Need I remind you, I was by myself, save for the elderly, well-dressed gentleman in the seat next to me—who looked as if he'd just unwillingly watched a hunt scene on *Animal Planet*. If the plane had crashed at that very moment, I think I would have been happier. If we had accidentally flown through the Bermuda Triangle, I would have been less traumatised.

On a good note, I got the product. A heck-of-sized maternity pad that had to last me the remainder of the ten-hour flight. (For anyone wondering if this was all worth it, the concert was brilliant. Would have bled a million more times for it. Would have told a million more old men that I was on my period if it meant experiencing that concert again.)

Alas, there is something to take from this. Period owners: do not forget your products whatever you are doing, wherever you are going—unless being called out on a ten-hour flight is something that really lights your fire.

Periods are never going to be my favourite thing—I dread them every month and curse my uterus for making itself known for a week every twenty-eight days—but learning how to work with them is one of the biggest things we can do for ourselves. Your periods don't have to be your best friend. Being period positive doesn't mean being excited that you experience one. But learning about your body, about menstruation, and learning to take care of yourself means they don't have to hold you back.

PERIOD KIT MUST-HAVES

- ★ a cute bag to store your period kit in—a pencil case or make-up bag works perfectly
- ★ pain medication or pain management products
- ★ period products—period underwear, pads and so on
- ★ extra underwear
- ★ wet wipes.

Dating and relationships

When I was twelve years old, I was abruptly taught about adulthood when Mum suggested we go bra shopping because my 'body was changing'. She was fibbing a bit—my body was about as curvy as a flounder (the fish, not the one from *The Little Mermaid*—google it). Despite the other girls in my class having long been wearing bras and spending recesses and bathroom breaks talking about cup sizes, bra shopping was not and, quite frankly, is still not necessary for me. Mum knew that, of course, but she assumed it would be a fun activity. She thought that like so many other kids my age, I'd think the idea of going bra shopping, make-up shopping and 'grown-up' shopping would be exciting.

Alas, I did what anyone with half a brain would do in my situation: I cried. I did not want things to change. I did not want to be a woman. I wanted to remain a little girl. Change was completely and entirely out of the question.

When I was thirteen, a boy from my church youth group announced that he liked me. I didn't respond (as in, I truly did not say a word—I shut my mouth, turned and walked away). And, then, you guessed it: I cried.

⚠ Sexual assault, PTSD

Love, relationships and boys have long terrified me, and rationally so after a horrible experience with a man as a little girl. This was a lot more than just a little girl scared of change, a little girl who just didn't really fancy the idea of adulthood. This was a little girl petrified of what it meant to be an adult because the one 'adult' experience she had had was full of fear and was not supposed to happen.

It is why relationships terrified me: I never wanted that to happen again. And it's why the idea of growing curves and boobs scared me—I saw the other girls my age beginning to be sexualised by the boys in my class once their bodies started to change, and I was frightened of the same thing happening to me.

Every therapist I have been to since I was seven has told both me and my parents that I may never want to be in a romantic or sexual relationship, that I may be repulsed entirely by the idea of intimacy, and this is a normal response to the trauma of child sexual abuse. For years, I would leave the room whenever there was an intimate scene in a film, or when teachers discussed sexual health and wellbeing. Even the ideas of consensual intimacy and loving relationships terrified me. My voice and ability to consent had been taken away in a home that I trusted, so how could I ever be sure they wouldn't be taken away again? How did I know if *anything* was safe?

Whenever anyone asked, or family members joked about me being in a relationship or having a boyfriend, it would be put to a halt with a firm, 'No, I am never getting married. I am never kissing anyone. I am never having babies.' And it wasn't something I was necessarily sad about; it was something I simply considered to be factual. I didn't want anyone, I knew I could never trust anyone, and that was okay. It was what it was.

Alas, as I grew older, the idea of finding someone to call my own began to get more appealing. I didn't particularly want a relationship in that moment, but when I looked to my future, it was with someone by my side—in a fantasy world, I figured, if I could work out a way to ensure that I was safe.

I knew the dangers of dating, both as a woman and as an autistic woman. Dating is significantly riskier for autistic women, with 78 per cent of them being sexually assaulted in their lives. Society's ideals of being a woman affect us all to some extent. All women are taught to obey, to conform, to act in an agreeable manner; we're taught that being tiny and vulnerable is wanted and valued. For autistic women, who have had to mask and take on a new persona to fit in, these standards can take over our entire beings. We're master maskers, we're chameleons, and we often take things to extremes, even when it's to our own detriment.

Another thing that can make relationships dangerous and difficult for autistic women is a lack of sexual knowledge. Comprehensive sex education and information can be woefully inaccessible, and we often, devastatingly, view abuse and mistreatment as 'normal' due to the excessive bullying we endured during our younger years. We also have a strong need for acceptance, and we struggle to predict other people's behaviours. Dating is difficult and often scary for everyone, I'm sure. Dating as an autistic woman, though, has far more challenges, and is far more terrifying.

Just because these challenges exist, however, doesn't mean that finding a relationship (if you desire one—for a long time I believed I was asexual, and that is entirely fine, too) is impossible. Finding a partner whom you feel safe with and who respects you is possible. So, how do we do this? How do we disabled people ensure that we're safe, that we're valued, that we're loved in our relationships?

I'm not an expert by any means. I've had minimal experience on the relationship front and, as previously stated, once ran a mile whenever sex and relationships were discussed. But I do know that one of the most important things in relationships is respect. Respect for each other and respect for you—for *all* parts of you.

I'm often asked when the right time is to tell someone you're seeing that you're neurodivergent or disabled. The answer to that is: as soon as you feel comfortable, and the sooner the better. While this may not mean literally introducing yourself as neurodivergent while you're announcing your name, it does mean discussing it sooner rather than later. This may seem an odd way to find potential partners, but I've come to the conclusion that if someone is going to be scared off when you bring up your neurodiversity, your disability, or anything else that may be different about you, that is someone you absolutely do not want to be with in the first place. Good riddance.

DISABLED/INTER-ABLED RELATIONSHIPS

Navigating a relationship can be difficult, regardless of whether or not you're neurodivergent. However, when you're a disabled person, finding healthy, loving, respectful relationships often comes with more challenges. What are we supposed to look for? What are red flags to steer clear of? How do we know when a relationship is toxic?

Red flags:

- ★ they have a hero mentality for choosing to date a disabled person
- ★ they are impatient with you
- ★ they discourage you from sharing or speaking up about your disability due to embarrassment and insecurity

→

- ★ they belittle your experience
- ★ they stigmatise or fetishise your disability
- ★ they don't listen to you
- ★ they victimise themselves—'It's hard for me to date someone disabled'
- ★ they gaslight you—'It's not that bad', 'If you just tried harder . . .', 'You need to stop [insert action], people are going to think you're crazy'
- ★ they exclude you from their circles
- ★ they refuse to acknowledge your disability
- ★ the neurodivergent/disabled partner uses their disability as an excuse for poor behaviour.

Green flags:

- ★ they do research to better understand your position
- ★ they don't make you feel like a burden
- ★ they show compassion
- ★ they encourage your special interests, hyper-fixations, stims and so on
- ★ you openly communicate with each other
- ★ they have a willingness to learn, change and grow
- ★ it doesn't feel like there's a hierarchy—you are both on the same level and show respect as equals
- ★ they are understanding of your needs.

When I first met my partner and told him I was autistic, his immediate response was to do a dive deep and search 'dating an autistic girl' on the internet—bless his soul. He was determined to find anything he possibly could that might help him understand, give him answers about what kind of traits he could expect to encounter, or how other people have managed relationships between people with different abilities, known as inter-abled relationships. Likewise, I began to google everything I could on how to be in a relationship—point-blank, period.

Several factors came to light. First of all, the dating advice that I discovered online was horribly ableist:

'Don't tell them you're autistic because it'll make them run away.'
'Learn how to act neurotypical.'
'Consider yourself lucky if someone chooses to date you.'

The overall impression was that inter-abled relationships were unequal, that disabled people do not and should not get a say, and that safety, communication and consent are privileges, rather than rights. All of which is complete and utter hogwash, and I happily (and thankfully) chose to ignore it. Babe, if you need to change and hide your being to appeal to a potential partner, they are *not* the sort of person you ever want to associate with. Kick 'em to the kerb. Block them. Leave them on 'read'.

One thing that I did notice pop up frequently in my research, and something that I'd learned through my years of reading, watching fairytale movies and from my own parents, was the importance of 'communication'. This incredibly vital concept is one that neurotypicals take great joy in both using and understanding but was a foreign concept to me. What these articles failed to communicate (ironically) was that every human being communicates differently and interprets communication differently—something my autistic brain had also failed to pick up within my twenty-three years of life.

And, boy, was this a key point to miss.

Picture this: me, going about my business, happy to be in an almost fairytale-perfect relationship, except that almost daily my butthead of a boyfriend blurted out odd demands and phrases, saying things that were, quite frankly, utterly outlandish and entirely unsolicited—including demands for me to take my clothes off, wolf whistles, and suggesting daily that I join him in the shower. I didn't choose to challenge him on these because I knew the sort of person he was, that he wouldn't ever say those sorts of things to intentionally make me uncomfortable. Perhaps it was just a 'male' thing, I thought.

In hindsight, this wasn't my smartest moment—one should never stay silent in a situation that feels uncomfortable. I ignored the behaviour, often just saying 'no' or telling him to 'bugger off'.

After growing sick and tired of these unsolicited opinions, my stomach twisting every time the person I adored made these comments, and speaking nothing of it for far too long, I finally spoke up. Three hours into the discussion, nothing had been resolved. It was at this point in the argument that I finally spoke up about what I had been feeling for months—that I wasn't ready for what I presumed was a legitimate daily request for something that I had told him multiple times I did not want.

Almost comically fast, my partner's sadness subsided and he laughed a little, leaving me incredibly confused. What followed was a gentle discussion as he explained what had been happening. While there had been communication between us, it had been in two entirely different languages. Alas, 'tone', as I have come to discover, is a valuable tool within neurotypical society, and one that I, as an autistic human, hadn't consciously considered.

Apparently, neurotypical people enjoy an odd, playful, loving, 'sarcastic' type of tone, and they call it 'flirtation'. *Apparently*, it's supposed to make one feel desirable, self-confident, loved and wanted. It's done without genuine expectation and is instead offered up as a form of gentle, light-hearted play and teasing, and should not be met with a blunt rejection and a monotonous 'rack off'. My partner explained that flirting was his way of showing love, appreciation and desire. He was using verbal communication to express intimacy.

Communication is vital. What is more vital, is making sure you and your partner (or anyone, for that matter) are communicating in the same language.

While there are struggles, there are also many beautiful positives about relationships. My partner eagerly encourages all of the things that make me, me. When I hyper-fixate and ramble about my special interests, he listens with eager anticipation, and asks questions so I can continue to ramble—both of us well aware that I've already spieled all of this information to him on more than one occasion. When we're going to places that we both know have the potential to trigger my brain into sensory overload or meltdowns, he'll remind me to pack my headphones and stim toys and, once we're there, check in on me frequently. On bad days, I'll find my weighted blanket, a cup of tea and *Mr. Magorium's Wonder Emporium* or a National Geographic documentary set up waiting for me. And, likewise, when there are things that he needs support with, I play an equally large part in the relationship and help him.

Relationships go both ways and I have just as much to contribute as anyone else. Being disabled, neurodivergent, chronically ill or anything else that society deems as 'less than' does not mean you are incapable of having a mutually beneficial relationship. You are not a burden, and you are incredibly worthy of love, respect and a happy, healthy, safe relationship—no less so than anyone else in this world.

Relationships may be something important to you or they may be something that you don't care for at all. Perhaps you only want certain types of relationships, and certain aspects of relationships. Whatever that may be, it's your right to feel safe and loved in the ways that you need.

And, of course, if something doesn't feel right, it's probably not. If there are issues, if you're uncomfortable, if there's doubt, there is a problem somewhere. The most important thing you can do is value yourself enough to speak up when something doesn't feel right.

Allowing behaviour to continue and accepting disappointment, hurt and sadness, regardless of the intent or the reason behind it, should never be accepted. A relationship is supposed to make you feel safe, loved and valued, and compromising those things for the sake of temporary comfort should never be the goal. If a relationship is a chapter you would like to have in your story, then you deserve your fairytale romance.

A NOTE FROM MY PARTNER

A relationship is the coming together of two stories. In our case, it is a love story between a neurodivergent person and a neurotypical person. You've heard a lot from me about our relationship so I thought it only right to hand the pencil to my partner to share his side.

After spending the better part of a day scouring the web for help when it came to dating someone on the spectrum, I knew very little. Most of what was online wasn't very specific to dating someone autistic, but instead was advice that would apply to any relationship. There are a few things that I did find out on my search that were appreciated—the first being the importance of comfort, and the sensory issues that may come with an autistic mind.

Our first date was at her house, a place she felt comfortable in. A place where it was quiet (sometimes), where she knew the people, where the lights weren't going to be 'loud' (as the internet phrased it). I requested that we wear comfortable clothes, knowing that she'd likely wear her flower and glitter. But it wasn't about her clothing choices, it was about being very clear early on that comfort and safety were my top priorities—in all aspects. I remember being afraid to ask about 'her condition'. Back then, all my training had taught me that 'she has autism' and not that 'she is autistic'. And my actions were guided by my language choices. I spent months trying to figure out what she could handle and what she couldn't. I had to decipher her preferences and sensory difficulties on my own until I realised it was not only fine to ask but also appreciated.

You're committed to the person, and why wouldn't you be. Their particular brand of neurodivergence is an important part of who they are and why you love them. You want to have an understanding of their limits and what you can do to help manage them. If I'm using the blender, power tools, or making a loud noise I give her notice, and pass over her noise-cancelling headphones. If she's been sitting here writing this book for too long, I remind her to take a break. If she's getting overwhelmed by the amount she has on in a week, we sit down and make a calendar and set clear, attainable goals that set her up for success. If we're out at a social event, I'll periodically ask, 'You doing okay?'—often just asking will put her at ease. At other times we may leave the situation for a minute before returning (which you'll be happy to know has been completely acceptable among family, friends and work colleagues).

Every now and again I'll see the ghost of Chloé. That's not meant to be derogatory in any way, it's simply the best way to describe what I see. She's expressionless, doesn't have any of her usual pep, and I can almost see the edges of the mask she so weakly defends herself with. It's important to know that there will be days like these. For Chloé, it's sometimes random (though, I'm sure it's not to her) but usually happens when she's physically run down,

→

finished a long period with a full schedule, been very upset and probably a few other causes I'm yet to notice. There are times when she goes non-verbal, when she becomes frustrated with simply existing, when miscommunication can cause stress for the both of us, and sometimes when she'll shut down completely, leaving no room for recovery. Though, I've discovered that the more comfortable we grow together, the rarer these moments become.

There are things you can do to help your person in times like this, though. For Chloé, it's quiet hugs, comfort films, weighted blankets, walks, swimming, alone time, etc. You know your person best, try to be helpful, but respect their need for space, too. I've come to learn that a need for space doesn't equal a lack of love.

There are so many things I love about dating someone autistic. I think the way she bounces, flaps and smiles so unashamedly when she's excited about something is beautiful. She's not embarrassed to be excited about a dusty old *Titanic* book, or a dinosaur blanket she's owned for weeks. I love how passionate she is about social justice, and how she'll fight with statistics and facts long after tears have started rolling—we've spent hours debating why we can't just print more money, why our context and world view may be different to others', or why there's no such thing as sustainable fishing. I didn't like fish that much anyway.

I love that she talks about her special interests with such passion and can tell me the same fact as though she only just heard it for the first time a moment ago. I love how we can be given the same problem, and she'll solve it immediately, and in a way so differently than I would have ever considered.

She doesn't care about social hierarchies, or social etiquette. If she disagrees with you, your friends or your family, you're likely to hear about it.

I also love that she knows she's different and embraces it. She doesn't pretend to be boring and normal; she's colourful, glitterful and just plain fun. She doesn't attempt to fit societal constructs or be anything she isn't, which means she's able to be entirely who she is, glitter and all. I know exactly who she is, everyone who meets her does. I know Chloé entirely, and it's a privilege to be with her.

Work

When I was fourteen, I started to see peers getting jobs and working, and was confused and unsure about what I was supposed to be doing in this regard. The school system and a society that pushes capitalism and a 'work as soon as you can' mentality made it seem natural for me to take a job. I decided to take a position at a local cafe that I frequented. What followed on my first day was a spilled coffee on a customer's lap, a panic attack at the sound of the coffee machine, and a call to Mum, begging her to pick me up. Then I chose to ghost the boss every day after that and simply never return. I knew in that single first shift that the workplace wasn't built for me.

In Australia, 31.6 per cent of autistic people are unemployed, three times the rate of those with other disabilities, and six times the rate of non-disabled Australians. Fifty-four per cent of unemployed autistic Australians have never held a paying job, despite often possessing skills, education, qualifications and the work ethic and drive to join the workforce. Of autistic people who are employed, more than half have stated that they want to be working more, and in more challenging roles, while 45 per cent report that their skills are far higher than needed for the job they are currently employed in. Twenty per cent of autistic Australians have lost jobs due to being autistic.

These statistics do not reflect the work ethic or skills of autistic people, but are the result of work being inaccessibile to them, a lack of understanding of autism, and a refusal to accommodate differences in the workplace, even when this may be incredibly simple. The workforce has long been adamantly anti-disability, anti-autism and anti-anyone who doesn't fit a specific profile—hiding racism, sexism and ableism behind job requirements and etiquette.

> 'Curly hair is simply unprofessional.'
> 'Working from home isn't an option.'
> 'Are you planning on having children in the future?'
> 'You're a liability.'
> 'This isn't a disability employment agency.'

Workplace discrimination is simply something we've had to live with. We've lived with women getting paid an average of 16.8 per cent less than men, and getting fired for being pregnant. We've lived with more than one in five disabled employees facing discrimination from their employers, and with Australia ranking the lowest among OECD countries for the relative income of disabled employees. Minority groups are consistently, continuously discriminated against, further segregated, and denied accommodation in the workplace. It's only when discriminatory behaviours affect a wider population and affect those in charge, those at the head of the pack, that they receive attention. They then get thrown into the wind, like they were never there in the first place, as though marginalised people haven't been forced out of the workplace prior to these changes.

The Covid-19 pandemic, for example, saw many people switch to working from home—something once seen as impossible in many jobs. With so much work now able to be done in different, alternative ways, these jobs can now accommodate people who were previously excluded. Alas, it took a global pandemic and the suffering of people who fit the social norm to finally prompt a search for alternative solutions.

It seems that if you're disabled, your suffering is acceptable and irrelevant. And still, even after a global pandemic forced us to make the workplace more accessible, our workforce remains adamantly un-sensory, un-autism, un-disability friendly. Jobs that require little to no social skills still expect candidates to have high social abilities upon application. Job interviewers reject autistic people, pushing them away, despite social skills having no connection to the job. People are judged on what they look like and sound like, rather than on what they can do. On paper, neurodivergence is an immediate red flag.

Despite this, autistic people have every ability to thrive within the workplace. There's a reason why so many of the top CEOs in the world are autistic, and why many of the most famous people in any given profession are autistic.

A typical nine-to-five is not the sort of job that my brain is built for, nor is it for many neurodivergent people. I'm incredibly fortunate that my entrepreneurial mindset and missions were well accepted and encouraged by my family. By the time I was sixteen, I had had three successful businesses.

My first business was family portrait photography. Every weekend I'd book hour-long slots, have Mum drive me to the local park or beach, and I'd photograph up to ten families a day. My second business was a jewellery company. With Mum's help, I made jewellery out of old Golden Books, scrabble letters and anything else I could find. I had a waitlist a mile long of people waiting to buy my pieces. And my third business was my character

FAMOUS AUTISTIC PEOPLE

- ★ Albert Einstein (scientist and mathematician)
- ★ Daryl Hannah (actor and environmentalist)
- ★ Tim Burton (director)
- ★ Henry Cavendish (scientist)
- ★ Charles Darwin (naturalist, biologist and geologist)
- ★ Bill Gates (co-founder of Microsoft)
- ★ Barbara McClintock (scientist and cytogeneticist)
- ★ Michelangelo (sculptor, painter, architect and poet)
- ★ Isaac Newton (mathematician, astronomer and physicist)
- ★ Tom Wiggins (musician)
- ★ Nikola Tesla (inventor)
- ★ Elon Musk (entrepreneur)
- ★ Leonardo da Vinci (artist and inventor)
- ★ Thomas Edison (inventor)
- ★ Ludwig van Beethoven (composer and pianist)
- ★ Temple Grandin (scientist)
- ★ Anthony Hopkins (actor)
- ★ Hans Christian Andersen (author)

entertainment company, where my Princess Anna costume not only helped me find my sparkle and move towards my current job as an actor and motivational speaker, but also jump-started my first large business pursuit. Through that company, I worked for charities such as the Make-A-Wish Foundation, the Wish Upon A Star Foundation and Red Nose Day. I had a dozen costumes, was fully booked every weekend and even had several employees.

I absolutely thrived as a business owner—making a wage and doing what I loved in a way that worked for me. The typical workplace doesn't suit me or my mind, and I know that if I hadn't been given the means and support to follow my dreams and find work in places that made me happy, I would be a part of that 31.6 per cent who are deemed unemployable.

I've lost work and been discriminated against for being autistic, even in my line of acting, advocacy and motivational speaking. I've been ridiculed by event owners who book me to talk for not offering my services for free, telling me that it's a disgrace that I charge because, since I'm disabled, I owe it to the community to work for free. You wouldn't think that would be the case when your main line of work is quite literally disability advocacy. Imagine, discriminating against an autistic person in autism advocacy. The cheek.

There've been several roles for television series or big-name presenter roles that I have auditioned for where the producers and casting agents excitedly announced and promote the fact that they wanted diverse people. They asked specifically for people with different backgrounds, whose voices hadn't been heard, and were eager to hear that I had a background in disability advocacy. After getting through multiple rounds of auditions, after speaking to casting directors and producers, and on more than one occasion even being offered the job, I was immediately turned away the moment I told them I was autistic. Sometimes this would be a subtle email or phone call with, 'Hey! We've decided to go with someone else due to a change of direction for the show.' Other times, it was an outright, 'We don't believe someone with autism will handle this sort of environment. It's best for you if we hire someone else.' *Yeah. Okay, Sia.*

I've had speaking gigs for which my job was literally to do nothing except share my story of being disabled and speak about ableism, accessibility and difference. But the event organisers would speak to me like an infant, and event participants would roll their eyes when I spoke up because I was a disabled person with lived experience, rather than a non-disabled 'expert'. Or neurotypical people would butt in and answer questions on my behalf because 'someone with autism wouldn't have the capacity to'.

Sensory issues, communication issues and society's refusal to implement easy changes to work conditions are huge issues, and are a large reason why the unemployment rate is disproportionately high for autistic people, despite them being some of the most talented people around when we're given the resources we need. However, our world runs on a capitalist standard of work requiring us to conform and fit and work in order to survive—a concept forced into us from the moment we're put into school, and drilled into us throughout our lives.

In his famous TEDx Talk entitled 'Do schools kill creativity?', Sir Ken Robinson stated, 'If we were to design an education system to kill creativity, we couldn't design one better than the one we already have.' Our society censures creativity and individuality, seeing forms of self-expression that do not fit into the tiny box of expectation as 'behavioural problems'.

In the late 1930s, an eight-year-old girl was condemned for being a problem student with suspected learning difficulties due to her inability to sit still and concentrate. That girl, Gillian Lynne, ended up being one of the world's most successful choreographers and dancers, choreographing hits such as Andrew Lloyd Webber's *Cats* and *The Phantom of the Opera*. This child was written off because she didn't fit into the black-and-white box of education, but her extraordinary talent superseded anything within that classroom.

At the age of twelve, a young boy overheard his teacher telling the school inspector that he was 'addled' and wouldn't be worth keeping in school any longer. He asked seemingly unnecessary questions, had poor math skills and was unable to concentrate. So, he was taken out of the system. That boy? Thomas Edison, one of the world's greatest inventors, who was also autistic.

Accessibility should not be praised; it should be expected.

Creative thinkers and neurodivergent minds are being let down by the education system, and then are unable to fulfil their potential in the workplace. We're given next to no resources to help us with our transition into adulthood, leaving neurodivergent people feeling lost, confused and often unemployable. We have a constantly changing economic landscape, where socialising and people skills have become key criteria for most jobs, even when they aren't part of the job itself. We're forced to compete against neuro-typical and able-bodied people in a society that has demonised and condemned disabled people throughout our entire lives. We're constantly ridiculed and belittled and pushed out of the workplace. It's not good enough.

As an actor, I'm in a line of work that is inherently anti-autism. Hollywood and the media play instrumental roles in creating and maintaining false stereotypes of neurodivergence. Both in front of and behind the camera, autistic people are treated as less than. As characters in film and television, we're used as props, and for comedy and shock value—*'At least my life isn't that bad'*. The 5 per cent of disabled actors who are used in disabled roles (meaning that 95 per cent of disabled characters are played by able-bodied actors) are often treated horribly, without easily made accommodations. In this industry, marking my place has been incredibly difficult.

Advocating for yourself in the workplace (or anywhere) can be hard, particularly when society has taught us that self-advocacy in a workplace environment is not allowed. We're expected to put in the most work on minimum pay; we're expected to come in even when we're physically or mentally unwell. In a society that is constantly telling us to put our work before ourselves, doing the opposite can feel taboo and selfish. But, advocacy and your voice are the most important tools you have to combat this mindset.

Now, I refuse to accept jobs that refuse to cater to me. I'll confidently tell bosses of production companies when they're acting in a way that's bigoted, ableist or unethical, and have no fear of publicly calling out places that refuse to change. I deserve to be valued as a worker, as an autistic person and as a human. On sets where I have been cast in a show, crew members are educated about autism, and they understand, accept and accommodate the different needs of not just me, but everyone on that set. Clapperboards that were once deafening to me are now closed quietly, or I'm given the opportunity to move and cover my ears. My noise-cancelling headphones are always nearby and handy. I'm not considered less than; I'm not considered more work. I'm simply considered another actor.

I'm in my dream job now. I spend my life as an advocate and ambassador. I'm an actor. I'm a musician. I'm an author. I'm thriving in my line of work because it's *my line of work.* It's what makes sense to me, and I've been given the resources and the accessibility I need in order to make it happen.

I could never work in an office job or be a doctor. I could never hold the majority of common jobs because the work sector is still not designed with autistic people in mind. But in my work? In the areas where I sparkle? Hell, I'm the best there is.

I grew up with teachers telling me I would never amount to anything, with a mum who cried after my diagnosis because she thought it meant I would never be successful, and then a mum whose mindset changed to, *She'll never hold a job, but as long as she's happy, it's okay.* But, because I was given the resources that I needed, because I demanded accessibility rather than tiptoed around it, I'm now thriving.

I'm an autistic human being, and I wholly believe that while society may continue to tell me that I am worthless, unemployable and a burden, that my autism is *why* I am successful. There's a reason why so many of the greats, the doers, the top people in absolutely any field are autistic. I mean that. Go look. Choose a topic of interest and investigate the people at the top.

When we're in our areas, when we're not given societal, capitalist limitations, we absolutely thrive. We're the doers of the world. We're the makers of the world. We are instrumental in this world. And it's time workplaces, and we ourselves, see that.

Embracing the future

On the night before my thirteenth birthday, I refused to go to sleep because I thought that if I just didn't fall asleep, the morning wouldn't come. I wouldn't be considered a teenager; I'd stay twelve. I'd stay a child. Clearly, it did not work. (Don't bother trying; you'll be heavily disappointed.)

On my eighteenth birthday, my parents threw a huge surprise party with nearly a hundred people (some of whom I didn't even know). They spent way more than they should have, buying special food and beautiful cakes and preparing speeches and buying hundreds of dollars' worth of Tinkerbell decorations.

Eighteen is meant to be a 'coming of age'. It's supposed to be exciting, the next chapter in your life, the beginning of a new adventure. And yet, when they opened the door and revealed the extravagant birthday party suited for a Disney princess, all I could do was cry. I slept in my parents' bed that night, once again fearful of what tomorrow would bring.

Every single birthday, I've silently sat, hoping and praying that Peter Pan would come and take me away. That he'd come into my

I'm an autistic human being, and I wholly believe that while society may continue to tell me that I am worthless, unemployable and a burden, that my autism is *why* I am successful.

open window, laughing and telling me this was all some huge, insane prank and then he'd whisk me off to Neverland, where my biggest worries would be pirates and crocodiles and mermaids, and the fears of growing up would become a faraway dream.

When I turned twenty, I grew fearful once again. I felt a whole new set of unmeetable expectations fall on my shoulders—from society, from myself—telling me who and what I should be. I was fearful about no longer being a teenager, about no longer being addressed as a girl but as a woman.

Now I'm in my twenties, and I'm not going to lie: growing older still petrifies me to no end. Life as a whole—the vastness of life, the littleness of life—is so bewildering and disconcerting. But I've now come to the show-stopping realisation that I cannot stop time. I cannot deny the inevitable fact that the world keeps turning, that getting older happens. And while the thought still occasionally sends my tummy into knots, I think I've also realised that growing older doesn't necessarily mean growing up. It just means being able to do so much more, that you have *lived* so much more.

Recently, I came across a journal entry I wrote the day before my twentieth birthday. It reads:

> *Dear Diary,*
> *I'm so proud of myself and what I'm starting to do. I can't believe that I went into the city for the first time by myself to see Little Mix! And I did something really, really big and exciting that I never thought I would be able to do by myself!*

What was the really big, really exciting thing, I hear you ask with bated breath, leaning into the book with extravagant wonder? I caught an Uber to BIG W. A round trip of about 2 kilometres.

I was so, so bloody proud of myself that day. I remember getting into that Uber with the biggest smile on my face, beaming from ear to ear, and walking into BIG W with my chin up and my chest out, as if I was Elsa in the power ballad stage of 'Let It Go'. I felt like a million dollars. No one could *touch* me. I was *that bitch*.

I had told the driver a grand total of four times in the five-minute trip that it was my first time catching an Uber. I smiled smugly and saw a look of shock on the driver's face, absolutely certain it was one of *wow, how grown up*.

Come to think of it, that particular weekend was full of things that were big, and new, and different. It was the first weekend I ever spent without my family, in a city that wasn't my own—mind you, it *was* only fifty minutes away from home. I remember being so excited, and happy and proud that I was at the Little Mix concert without anybody else, that I was meeting people and making friends and doing 'grown-up things'. It was the first time of many when 'growing up' wasn't a negative in my vocabulary.

You are capable of so many amazing things when you open up to the possibilities of change, when you allow yourself to grow, instead of being scared of it. Growing up doesn't have to be taken as, *I'm losing the ability to live life in the safety of what I've always known*. Instead, it can mean, *I'm gaining the ability to go on adventures. To do more, to see more, to be more.* And that's cool. That's so goddamn cool.

I'm an adult now, and that's okay. That's exciting. How bloody beautiful that I can sit here and say that I've made it this far when so many people do not. I have a job that I love more than anything. I have a partner I adore and who adores me. I've travelled the world solo. I'm doing things that I am only capable of doing because I've spent enough years on this Earth to be considered a grown-up. I'm doing things that I can only do because I am a grown-up.

But I still cuddle a teddy every single night when I'm falling asleep, and eagerly collect more when I see one in an op shop or a garage sale, particularly if it's fluffy, looks sad and looks like it needs to come home with me. I still climb onto Dad's lap for a cuddle when I have a problem, and cry in Mum's arms when the world gets too much. I still name all of my toy horses, and beg my little sister to play Barbies with me even though her nine-year-old self is 'far too grown-up to be playing pretend . . . but don't worry Chloé, I'll play with you'. I still watch my favourite childhood films again and again, and prefer them far more than any film created for my own age. My bedroom is still filled with my little whozits and whatzits and thingamabobs that make me happy, despite them potentially not being overly aesthetically pleasing. I still enjoy playing dress-up, and regularly put on my princess dresses just because.

There's a line in *Mr. Magorium's Wonder Emporium* that I remind myself of whenever my heart pangs with fear about the future: 'We must face tomorrow, whatever it may hold, with determination, joy and bravery.' It's one of my favourite quotes in the whole world, and it has stuck so incredibly deeply within me, making me feel a little less terrified about the idea of growing up.

It's okay to be scared of the future. The future is uncertain, and ever changing, and so often out of our hands. But fear doesn't have to be a bad thing. It can mean that we're about to do something brave, and magnificent, and *new.* Nobody ever made a difference inside of their comfort zone. Nothing *grows* inside of a comfort zone.

The future isn't something to be scared of. It's something to be celebrated, to be thankful for, to go into with joy and wonder and excitement.

CONCLUSION

Finding Your Happily Ever After

I was so sure, for so long, that a Happily Ever After wasn't in the cards for me, that those pages of my book had been ripped out, gone, cast away. That I would be stuck in an endless, eternal loop of dragon-fighting until my story eventually came to an anti-climactic, disappointing, dissatisfying end. But, I, Chloé Hayden, have found my Happily Ever After.

The thing that I've learned about fairytales is that every single one of them, no matter the journey, *does* have a Happily Ever After. No story can exist without it, no fairytale can be completed without it. All heroes, all protagonists, get their Happily Ever After.

When we read and watch and engage with fairytales, we allow ourselves to sit through the bad and tough Once Upon a Time and Adventure stages because we know that there will inevitably be a good ending. When our favourite characters deal with issues, we know that good will ultimately prevail, that the cinematic music will begin, and the character will exhale a triumphant breath, hold their chin high and overcome both the literal and metaphorical evil that has been stopping them from getting to the end of their journey. We persist with watching fairytales because we know that just around the river bend, just past the elephant graveyard, just over the rainbow, there's a Happily Ever After waiting to be discovered.

Simba reached his Happily Ever After. A kind warthog, a sassy meerkat and an ADHD-coded monkey helped him to see that he was so, so much more than what he had been told throughout his life. Because of this, he had the courage, strength and support to go back to Pride Rock, defeat Scar and gain his rightful title as the King of Africa.

Genie reached his Happily Ever After. A kind homeless boy who made him a promise, and stuck to it, meant that Genie got his number one wish. He was free.

Quasimodo reached his Happily Ever After. After twenty years of being hidden away in a bell tower and being ridiculed by society, he was accepted for who he was. He grew confident, independent, happy. He found love. He was accepted, not just by the city but, most importantly, by himself.

I, Chloé Sarah Hayden, reached my Happily Ever After. Because I embraced my different, because I refused to conform to society's unattainable expectations, because I have a network of people who love and support me to be me, I accepted all parts of who I was, and I discovered that being *me* was the most beautiful, powerful, important thing I could do.

Peter Pan never came for me, and I've decided now that it's okay to close the bedroom window. I don't need a fantasy land of pirates and pixies to create my own fairytale down here on Earth. It's okay, Peter Pan. I'm happy right where I am.

Your life is a fairytale. And you are its protagonist.

We all have different Once Upon a Times, different Adventures—dragons to fight, villains to overcome—and different Happily Ever Afters, because our stories are all different, the characters in them are different, and we even play different characters when our fairytales intersect with those around us. Life is one huge 'choose your own adventure' story, and the most magical part? You are in control.

It's true that, unlike fairytales, our lives aren't always so linear. There are infinite stories, infinite tales, within the world and within ourselves. We may travel between Adventure stages and Happily Ever Afters and Once Upon a Times multiple times. Our lives are a constant cycle of stories and chapters. Our lives involve series and sequels and trilogies.

I've lived a million Once Upon a Times, I've fought a million dragons, and I've closed a million Happily Ever Afters. Every day

I eagerly pick up the book of my fairytale, going into a new Adventures, thinking *What can my life become today?* rather than fear *What terrible thing will be laced in these pages?*

The Adventure stage is often laced with struggles, but it also contains our greatest learning and discoveries. If it wasn't for the rocky roads and treacherous tracks, growth would be impossible. The strongest roots come from the hardest grounds, and linear tracks become incredibly boring.

Every single one of us is different, and without a doubt, that is why the world is such a beautiful, wonderful place. Some people are better at hiding their differences, or society is better at embracing them. But just because society believes something, doesn't mean it's true, or that we don't have the power to change it. Because the thing is, different isn't a bad thing.

I no longer care for society's opinions and have learned that we have the choice to focus on what and whose opinions and views matter to us. (Hint: a culture created for the benefit of abled, typical, heteronormative, Caucasian, upper-class men will never be a culture that benefits me, so why should I allow it to matter to me?) I no longer fear the eyes of others, or feel that someone's judgement is my own personal problem, or is representative of who I am. I've taught myself that my mind, my differences and my identity are valid, and important, and hold value. I've come to this realisation after years of being taught otherwise.

I had my sidekicks. There was Wendy, who taught me when I was at my most vulnerable that my Happily Ever After would come. My parents stood right beside me and fought every dragon that entered my path until I was old enough to handle the sword (and even then, will still wield their own when I need an extra army). I had the old ladies at camera club, and the other volunteers at Riding for the Disabled, and the people I go to concerts with, and the old cowboys, and the now hundreds of thousands of neurodivergent people with whom I've built this incredible online community.

I had my tribe, and I made my tribe, and it's mine.

As you close these pages and continue your own fairytale, let the following guide you:

★ Find your support group—your people are out there, your chosen family who will make you feel loved, and valued, and safe.

★ Know your worth—speak up, stand up, be courageous because you deserve to live your most whole, beautiful life. You are the author of your fairytale, so don't let anyone or anything take that pen from you.

★ Find your eye sparkle—you have one, I promise you, and when you begin to use it, it's going to be wonderful.

★ Know that different doesn't mean less—there is so much beauty in difference, and when we begin to embrace it, our world is going to be so, so beautiful.

We are all living in a fairytale. Our lives are occasions, and it's time to rise to them.

If there's anything you take from this book, let it be this: embrace who you are. You are exactly who you're supposed to be.

Acknowledgements

No one in a fairytale is complete without their sidekicks, and I am no different. Just as Peter Pan could not fly without Tinkerbell's pixie dust, there are so many dust makers in my story.

To Dad, my Mufasa, you are my greatest teacher and supporter, the most brilliant fairytale of a father to ever exist. Thank you for encouraging me to reach higher and to do and be more than I ever believed possible, for never accepting anything less than the best version of myself. Thank you for being so involved, instead of just listening to my eccentric ideas and nodding at the right times, and for giving your advice and opinions, and for enthusiastically adding in your own—we may joke about giving you credit for what I have created, but I truly would not be where I am today if it wasn't for you.

To Mum, thank you for being my Sarabi. Thank you for advocating for me, for the fierceness you show—metaphorically crashing down school gates, dragging teachers by their earlobes to principals' offices, calling people out who have done wrong by me—in the name of protecting me. Thank you for the countless bowls of dahl and Vego bars, for advocating for me when I forget to, for being my greatest cheerleader. I can fight my own battles, but it sure helps when there's a warrior standing behind me.

To my partner, Dylan, thank you for creating spreadsheets to help me manage my time while writing this book, reminding me to take breaks, and endless cups of ginger tea, weighted blankets and Barbie movies. You helped me see that I was more than worthy of a fairytale ending.

Thank you to Kenpa and Nanny because, when the world got too much, I knew your arms would always be open for me to run into. I think you would have liked this book, Nanny. You were so excited to hear about what I was up to and the first to call to listen to my rambles. More than anything I would love to call you one more time and tell you everything.

Thank you to Lou Johnson, who I was positive was a scammer when she sent me a DM telling me she wanted me to write my story for Murdoch Books. And to her incredible daughter Ruby, who was the reason Lou reached out in the first place. It seems that magical genies don't just come in the form of blue giants. You made my biggest wishes come true. And, to the entire Murdoch team, including Editorial Manager Julie Mazur Tribe and Head of Marketing and Publicity Sue Bobbermein, and freelance editor Joanne Holliman, who were my Flora, Fauna and Merryweather. You are the most brilliant fairy godmothers an author could ask for.

To everyone in the autism organisations who held my hand as I started walking this path almost a decade ago, most particularly those at Yellow Ladybugs and Amaze, thank you for helping me find and raise my voice, and being my greatest supporters from day one of this incredible journey.

Many meltdowns may have been had in the creation of this book if it wasn't for the world's greatest weighted blanket, tear drier and cuddle toy the world has ever known, my best friend and dog, Matilda.

I would also not have the knowledge that my mind, in all that it is, is exactly as it needs to be if it weren't for my first sidekick, my Year 4 teacher, Wendy.

To my therapist, my personal assistant and all the people who keep me going and my head screwed on, I don't know what sort of magical spells you have under your capes, but you've changed my life a million times over. Thank you.

Sadly, if I sat down to list all my sidekicks, I fear the acknowledgements would be longer than the book. You know who you are, and I am eternally, ever grateful that you are a part of my story.

Most importantly, thank you to the autistic and disabled community. Thank you to those who paved the way before me and made that path a little wider, a little more worn and clearer of brambles. Thank you for showing me there was a rocket ship full of people waiting to welcome me. And, when the time came, thank you for allowing me to take control of my own rocket ship and riding in it with me. This book isn't just my story, it's all of ours.

May we all go into tomorrow, whatever it may hold, with determination, joy and bravery.

Support Resources

There are many organisations that offer advice, help, social engagement and other services for neurodivergent people. This list is a good place to start, although it is not exhaustive and you will probably find places that can assist you closer to home. Organisations marked with ** offer international support.

Australia

ADHD

ADDults with ADHD

Authoritative information, publications and services to support adults with ADHD and their families and friends. Events include quarterly ADHD afternoons led by speakers and a chance to meet and chat with others.
adultadhd.org.au

ADHD Australia

Support groups, research and a newsletter sharing the latest information and resources for ADHD folk and their families.
adhdaustralia.org.au

AUTISM

Amaze

Information and resources for autistic people, including workshops, online resources and an autism helpline via phone, email or live chat.
amaze.org.au • *Helpline: 1300 308 699*

I CAN Network

Professional development workshops and campaigns to increase autism understanding.
icannetwork.online

Yellow Ladybugs

Support and informal events for autistic girls and gender-diverse individuals between the ages of five and sixteen.
yellowladybugs.com.au

COMPLEX TRAUMA

Blue Knot

Phone counselling, resources and workshops for adults affected by childhood trauma and abuse. Also educates and trains people to support survivors.
blueknot.org.au • Helpline and Redress Support Service: 1300 657 380 • National Counselling and Referral Services—Disability: 1800 421 468

EATING DISORDERS

The Butterfly Foundation

Support for all people affected by eating disorders and negative body image—the person with the illness, their family and their friends.
butterfly.org.au

GENERAL MENTAL HEALTH

Beyond Blue

Information and support to help everyone in Australia achieve their best possible mental health.
beyondblue.org.au • 1300 224 636

Black Dog Institute

A transnational research institute that aims to reduce the incidence of mental illness and the stigma around it, to actively reduce suicide rates and empower everyone to live the most mentally healthy lives possible.
blackdoginstitute.org.au

Embrace Multicultural Mental Health

Mental health and suicide prevention services for people from culturally and linguistically diverse backgrounds.
embracementalhealth.org.au

Headspace

The National Youth Mental Health Foundation, providing early intervention mental health services to twelve to twenty-five year olds, along with assistance in promoting the wellbeing of young people.
headspace.org.au

Kids Helpline

Australia's only free, private and confidential 24/7 phone and online counselling service for young people between the ages of five and twenty-five.
kidshelpline.com.au • 1800 551 800

Lifeline

National 24-hour crisis support and suicide prevention services.
lifeline.org.au • *13 11 14*

LGBTQIA+

QLife

Anonymous LGBTQIA+ peer support and referral for a range of issues, including sexuality, identity, gender, bodies, feelings or relationships. Free telephone and webchat delivered by trained LGBTQIA+ people.
qlife.org.au • *1800 184 527*

MINUS18

LGBTQIA+ resources, workplace training, school workshops and events for youth across Australia.
minus18.org.au

Switchboard

Peer-driven support and resources for members of the LGBTQIA+ community, their families, allies and the community.
switchboard.org.au

SEXUAL ASSAULT

1800RESPECT

Free and confidential support 24 hours a day, every day, for sexual assault, domestic and family violence counselling, information and referrals.
1800respect.org.au • *1800 737 732*

Bravehearts

Counselling and education for children and young people as well as parental support, training and research to combat issues associated with child sexual assault.
bravehearts.org.au • *1800 272 831*

Ireland/United Kingdom

ADHD

ADHD Foundation

Services, resources and events for autism, ADHD, dyslexia, dyspraxia, dyscalculia and Tourette's syndrome.
adhdfoundation.org.uk

ADHD Ireland

Resources, support, events, social outings and a dedicated phone and email hotline for people with ADHD and their families and carers.
adhdireland.ie • *01 874 8349*

ADHD UK

Provides an online guide to support groups that span across the United Kingdom.
adhduk.co.uk

AUTISM

As I Am

A leading autism charity that offers training, education, support and resources.
asiam.ie

AUsome Training

A community organisation run by autistic people that offers in-person and online courses to address the inaccurate portrayal of autism. Also the home of AUsome Cork, an annual conference featuring autistic advocates who educate the general public about the needs of autistic people.
ausometraining.com

Autistic Inclusive Meets (AIM)

A not-for-profit autistic advocacy organisation created by autistic people that focuses on promoting autism acceptance, protesting against laws that harm autistic people and connecting the autistic community. Hosts weekly meetups and events for the autistic community, both in person and online.
autisticinclusivemeets.org

National Autistic Society

Support, guidance, diagnostic services, professional development and education and employment opportunities for autistic people.
autism.org.uk

EATING DISORDERS

Beat Eating Disorders

Information, advice and a supportive online community for those affected by eating disorders. They have helplines in England, Scotland, Wales and Northern Ireland that run 365 days per year.
beateatingdisorders.org.uk • *0808 801 0677*

Eating Disorders Association NI

Free and confidential support for anyone living with an eating disorder, their family, friends and carers, and for professionals working with eating disorders.
eatingdisordersni.co.uk

GENERAL MENTAL HEALTH

Childline

Free counselling for children and young people with any issue they may be confronting.
childline.org.uk • 0800 1111

Mind

Advice and support to empower anyone experiencing a mental health problem.
mind.org.uk • 0300 123 3393

National Suicide Prevention Helpline

A supportive listening service for anyone with thoughts of suicide.
nsphuk.org • 0800 689 5652

Samaritans

Free, confidential mental health support via phone or email.
samaritans.org • 116 123

SANEline

National out-of-hours helpline for mental health support.
sane.org.uk • 07984 967 708

Shout

Free, confidential mental health support 24/7 via text.
giveusashout.org • Text: 'shout' to 85258

LGBTQIA+

AKT

Support for LGBTQIA+ young people aged sixteen to twenty-five who are facing or experiencing homelessness or living in a hostile environment, helping them to stay safe in crisis situations, find emergency accommodation, access specialist support and develop skills and life goals.
akt.org.uk • 020 7831 6562

LGBT Ireland

Resources and local peer-support groups for LGBTQIA+ people and their families, also offering online chat functions and two helplines, one for general LGBTQIA+ and one for transgender family support.

lgbt.ie • *+1800 929 539*

Switchboard

Peer-driven support and resources for LGBTQIA+ people, their families, allies and the community.

switchboard.lgbt • *0300 330 0630*

SEXUAL ASSAULT

Safeline

Free, specialist, best-practice services for adults and children affected by or at risk of sexual violence.

safeline.org.uk • *01926 402 498*

The Survivors Trust

Counselling, therapeutic and support services for victims of rape, sexual violence and sexual abuse, including free, confidential helpline and live chat services.

www.thesurvivorstrust.org • *08088 010818*

Canada/United States of America

AUTISM

Autistic Inclusive Meets (AIM)

Services to support autism acceptance, protest against laws that harm autistic people, and connect the autistic community. Meetups and events for the autistic community, both in person and online.

autisticinclusivemeets.org/aim-usa

Autistics for Autistics Ontario (A4A)

Support to improve rights and opportunities for autistic Canadian people, especially in the areas of school inclusion, employment, housing and access to medical care.

a4aontario.com

Autistics United Canada

A disability rights organisation created by autistic people that focuses on building a community of autistic people while fostering autistic identity and pride. The Vancouver chapter has a mobile neurodiversity library with books about autism acceptance as well as fidget gadgets for autistic people.

autisticsunitedca.org

**Autistic Women and Nonbinary Network (AWN)

An autistic-led organisation that provides community, support and resources for autistic women, girls, nonbinary people and all others of marginalised genders. They also provide support for minority groups, such as autistic LGBTQIA+ people and autistic people of colour. AWN provides opportunities to connect the autistic community through networking, educational and social gatherings, autism acceptance events, book readings and autistic pride picnics.
awnnetwork.org

**Nonspeaking CommUnity Consortium

A not-for-profit organisation founded by nonspeaking autistic and other neurodivergent nonspeaking people and allies that promotes communication access and choice.
de-de.facebook.com/groups/nonspeakingcommunity/

ADHD

**ADDitude

A quarterly magazine and online resource for people living with ADHD, providing access to evidence-based information, free webinars, an online community and more.
additudemag.com

CHADD

Education, advocacy and support for children and adults living with ADHD and their families, as well as teachers and healthcare professionals.
chadd.org • 866-220-8098

LGBTQIA+

**GLAAD

Empowers the LGBTQIA+ community by sharing their stories, holding the media accountable for the words and images they present and helping grass-roots organisations communicate effectively.
glaad.org

**It Gets Better

An internet-based not-for-profit organisation with a mission to uplift, empower and connect lesbian, gay, bisexual, transgender and queer youth around the globe.
itgetsbetter.org

Trans Lifeline

Confidential peer support phone service run by trans people for trans and questioning peers. Trans Lifeline is a hotline offering direct emotional and financial support to trans people in crisis.
translifeline.org • *877-565-8860*

**The Trevor Project

Suicide prevention support for lesbian, gay, bisexual, transgender, queer and questioning youth. The toll-free Trevor Lifeline is a confidential service that offers trained counsellors, as well as resources, public education and research.
thetrevorproject.org • *866-488-7386*

EATING DISORDERS

National Eating Disorders Association (NEDA)

Support for people affected by eating disorders, including treatment options, support groups, events and helplines in the form of online chat, call and text.
nationaleatingdisorders.org • *800-931-2237*

SEXUAL ASSAULT

RAINN

Anti-sexual violence services, public education, public policy, consulting services and a national hotline in partnership with more than 1,000 local sexual assault service providers across the United States, offering online live chat and telephone helplines.
rainn.org • *800-656-4673*

GENERAL MENTAL HEALTH

National Suicide Prevention Lifeline

Free, 24/7 and confidential support for people in distress, as well as prevention and crisis resources, and best practices for professionals.
suicidepreventionlifeline.org • *800-273-8255*

TheHopeLine

Resources for people struggling with poor mental health, including suicide and mental health resources, email mentors, prayer, weekly personalised emails and live chat service.
thehopeline.com

Notes

Judy Singer quote at neurodiversity2.blogspot.com/p/what.html

Chapter 2: School

Up to 30 per cent of student in a class are neurodivergent: 'Neurodiversity and other conditions', ADHA Aware, adhdaware.org.uk/what-is-adhd/neurodiversity-and-other-conditions/; 'Fast Facts', National Center for Education Statistics, nces.ed.gov/fastfacts/display.asp?id=60

Forty-four per cent of autistic children change schools multiple times, 35 per cent will not continue past Year 10: S. Jones, M. Akram, N. Murphy et al., 'Australia's attitudes and behaviours towards autism; and experiences of autistic people and their families', Autism and Education, Research Report for AMAZE, 26 September 2018, amaze.org.au/wp-content/uploads/2019/06/Education-Community-Attitudes-and-Lived-Experiences-Research-Report_FINAL.pdf

Chapter 3: Sensory Issues, Stimming, Meltdowns, Shutdowns and Burnout

Sensory processing disorder affects between 5 and 16 per cent of children, and up to 95 per cent of autistic people: J.P. Owen, E.J. Marco, S. Desai et al., 'Abnormal white matter microstructure in children with sensory processing disorders', *Neurolmage: Clinical*, vol. 2, 2013, pp. 844–53, sciencedirect.com/science/article/pii/S2213158213000776; and L. Crane, L. Goddard, L. Pring, 'Sensory processing in adults with autism spectrum disorders', *Autism*, vol. 13, no. 3, May 2009, pp. 215–28, journals.sagepub.com/doi/abs/10.1177/1362361309103794

In almost 50 per cent of autistic children forced to stop stimming, met the diagnostic threshold for PTSD: H. Kupferstein, 'Evidence of increased PTSD symptoms in autistics exposed to applied behavior analysis', *Advances in Autism*, vol. 4, no. 3, January 2018, researchgate.net/publication/322239353_Evidence_of_increased_PTSD_symptoms_in_autistics_exposed_to_applied_behavior_analysis

Autistic people have a nine-fold increase of dying by suicide: T. Hirvikoski, E. Mittendorfer-Rutz, M. Bowman et al., 'Premature mortality in autism spectrum disorder', *British Journal of Psychiatry*, vol. 208, no. 3, pp. 232–38, 4 November 2015, pubmed.ncbi.nlm.nih.gov/26541693/

Chapter 4: Friends and Sidekicks

Forty-three per cent of autistic teenagers never interact with peers outside school, 54 per cent have never received phone calls, 50 per cent have never been invited to a party: P.T. Shattuck, G.I. Orsmond, M. Wagner et al., 'Participation in social activities among adolescents with an autism spectrum disorder', PLOS ONE, 14 November 2011, journals.plos.org/plosone/article?id=10.1371%2Fjournal.pone.0027176&fbclid=IwAR2fOd18P-JTezQXK-aHDhdntB51RcCF9hbUX5GQTW2BuCYLYnFfuD-VP0RnQ

Chapter 5: Mental Health

More than 50 per cent of people will struggle with a serious mental illness: R.C. Kessler, M. Angermeyer, J.C. Anthony et al., 'Lifetime prevalence and age-of-onset distributions of mental disorders in the World Health Organization's World Mental Health Survey Initiative', *World Psychiatry*, vol. 6, no. 3, October 2007, pp. 168–76, pubmed.ncbi.nlm.nih.gov/18188442/

Seventy-two per cent of autistic people also struggle with a comorbid mental illness: O. Leyfer, S. Folstein, S. Bacalman et al., 'Comorbid psychiatric disorders in children with autism: Interview development and rates of disorders', *Journal of Autism Developmental Disorders*, vol. 36, no. 7, October 2006, pp. 849–61, pubmed.ncbi.nlm.nih.gov/16845581/

Disabled people five times more likely to struggle with mental illness than able-bodied folk: R.A. Cree, C.A. Okoro, M.M. Zack et al., 'Frequent mental distress among adults, by disability status, disability type, and selected characteristics—United States 2018', *Morbidity and Mortality Weekly Report (MMWR)*, vol. 69, no. 36, September 2020, pp. 1238–43, pubmed.ncbi.nlm.nih.gov/32914770/

Disabled people die by suicide at five times the rate of non-disabled counterparts; autistic people nine times more likely to die by suicide: S. Cassidy, P. Bradley, J. Robinson et al., 'Suicidal ideation and suicide plans or attempts in adults with Asperger's syndrome attending a specialist diagnostic clinic: A clinical cohort study', *The Lancet Psychiatry*, vol. 1, no. 2, July 2014, pp. 42–47, dx.doi.org/10.1016/ S2215-0366(14)70248-2

Ninety per cent of sexual assault victims know the perpetrator: O. Brooks-Hay, M. Burman, L. Bradley et al., 'Evaluation of the Rape Crisis Scotland National Advocacy Project: Final Report 2018', The Scottish Centre for Crime and Justice Research, University of Glasgow, 2018, eprints.gla.ac.uk/187695/1/187695.pdf

Eighty per cent of intellectually disabled women have been sexually abused: T.C. Weiss, 'People with disabilities and sexual assault', *Disabled World*, 20 November 2012, disabled-world.com/disability/sexuality/assaults.php

Disabled people seven times more likely to be sexually assaulted: E. Harrell, 'Crime against persons with disabilities, 2009–2019: Statistical tables', US Department of Justice, Office of Justice Programs, Bureau of Justice Statistics, bjs.ojp.gov/content/pub/pdf/capd0919st.pdf?fbclid=IwAR2wGum2RZjaMDLrPape3h904OzayRQjv0MMSX1ubMTjM87hKpVRmpK878M

Children as young as three experience poor body image: 'Children as young as 3 unhappy with their bodies', Professional Association for Childcare and Early Years, 31 August 2016, pacey.org.uk/news-and-views/news/archive/2016-news/august-2016/children-as-young-as-3-unhappy-with-their-bodies/

Eighty-one per cent of ten year olds are afraid of being fat: A. Kearney-Cooke and D. Tieger, 'Body image disturbance and the development of eating disorders' in *The Wiley Handbook of Eating Disorders, Assessment, Prevention, Treatment, Policy, and Future Direction*, Wiley Online Library, ch. 22, pp. 283–96, 2015

At least 25 per cent of anorexia sufferers are autistic, and other studies suggest 52.5 per cent of anorexia suffers are autistic: H. Westwood and K. Tchanturia, 'Autism spectrum disorder in anorexia nervosa: An updated literature review', *Current Psychiatry Reports*, vol. 19, article 41, 2017, doi.org/10.1007/s11920-017-0791-9

Girls with ADHD four times more likely to suffer from an eating disorder: J. Biederman, S.W. Ball, M.C. Monuteaux et al., 'Are girls with ADHD at risk for eating disorders? Results from a controlled, five-year prospective study', *Journal of Developmental & Behavioral Pediatrics*, vol. 28, no. 4, August 2007, pp. 302–307, journals.lww.com/jrnldbp/Abstract/2007/08000/Are_Girls_with_ADHD_at_Risk_for_Eating_Disorders_.7.aspx

More than half of bulimia sufferers are thought to have ADHD: S. Ulfvebrand, A. Birgegard, C. Norring et al., 'Psychiatric comorbidity in women and men with eating disorders results from a large clinical database', *Psychiatry Research*, vol. 230, no. 2, December 2015, pp. 294–99, pubmed.ncbi.nlm.nih.gov/26416590/

Up to 10 per cent of anorexia sufferers die within the first ten years, 20 per cent after twenty years; only 30 per cent fully recover: *Anorexia nervosa: Australian treatment guide for consumers and carers, 2005*, Royal Australian and New Zealand College of Psychiatrists, 2005, www1.health.gov.au/internet/main/publishing.nsf/Content/publications-mentalhealth

Seventy per cent of autistic children have issues with food and eating: S. Dickerson Mayes and H. Zickgraf, 'Atypical eating behaviors in children and adolescents with autism, ADHD, other disorders, and typical development', *Research in Autism Spectrum Disorders*, vol. 64, August 2019, pp. 76–83, sciencedirect.com/science/article/abs/pii/S1750946719300595

It's believed that one in ten POTS patients has ADHD: E. Willingham, 'APA 2019—1 in 10 POTS patients is diagnosed with ADHD instead', Univadis from Medscape, 28 May 2019, univadis.co.uk/viewarticle/apa-2019-1-in-10-pots-patients-is-diagnosed-with-adhd-instead-672604

Eighty-five per cent of POTS patients are incorrectly diagnosed with poor mental health: 'Physician Patient Interaction in Postural Orthostatic Tachycardia Syndrome', Dysautonomia International Report, dysautonomia international.org/pdf/PhysicianPatientInteractionInPOTS.pdf

Twenty-five per cent of POTS patients can no longer work or attend school: B.P. Grubb, 'Postural tachycardia syndrome', *Circulation*, vol. 117, no. 21, 27 May 2008; pp. 2814–17, ahajournals.org/doi/full/10.1161/circulationaha.107.761643

Suicide is perceived as significantly more acceptable for the disabled: E.M. Lund, M.R. Nadorff, E.S. Winer et al., 'Is suicide an option?: The impact of disability on suicide acceptability in the context of depression, suicidality, and demographic factors', *Journal of Affective Disorders*, vol. 189, January 2016, pp. 25–35, pubmed.ncbi.nlm.nih.gov/26402344/

In the UK, suicide is the leading cause of early death in autistic people: J. Cusack, S. Shaw, J. Spiers, et al., 'Personal tragedies, public crisis: The urgent need for a national response to early death in autism', Autistica, United Kingdom, 2017, academia.edu/26687912/Personal_tragedies_public_crisis_The_urgent_need_for_a_national_response_to_early_death_in_autism

Autistic people more than nine times more likely to die by suicide: T. Hirvikoski, E. Mittendorfer-Rutz, M. Boman et al., 'Premature mortality in autism spectrum disorder', *The British Journal of Psychiatry*, vol. 208, no. 3, March 2016, cited in J. Cusack et al., 'Personal tragedies, public crisis', op cit.

Seventy per cent of autistic people have mental health conditions: ibid.; see also, Australian Advisory Board on Autism Spectrum Disorders, 'The interface between autism spectrum disorders and mental health: The ways forward', discussion paper, December 2012.

On average, lifespan of autistic person 26 years shorter than non-autistic person: T. Hirvikoski et al., 'Premature mortality in autism spectrum disorder', op cit.

In Australia, 49 per cent of autistic adults have immense difficulty accessing clinical mental health support: 'The Autism Dividend: Unleashing the skills, talent and opportunity of Australia's autistic community', Submission to the Senate Select Committee on Autism, Australian Autism Alliance, August 2020, australianautismalliance.org.au/wp-content/uploads/2020/09/comprehensive-submission-Australian-Autism-Alliance-Senate-Inquiry-into-Autism-Aug-2020.pdf

More than 90 per cent of autistic adults have challenges accessing health care, with 33 per cent completely unable to: 'The Autism Dividend', as above.

Suicide is the leading cause of death for Australians between fifteen and forty-four, 54 per cent experiencing poor mental health will not ask for help: Australian Institute of Health and Welfare, Australia's Health 2014, Australia's health series no. 14, Cat. No. AUS 178, Canberra.

More than 10 per cent with a chronic mental health condition die by suicide within ten years of diagnosis, chronic health condition increases odds by 363 per cent: University of Waterloo, 'Young people with chronic illness more likely to attempt suicide', *ScienceDaily*, 17 August 2017, sciencedaily.com/releases/2017/08/170817110905.htm

Suicide rates of Indigenous Australians almost double: Australian Bureau of Statistics, Causes of Death, Australia, 2015, 'Intentional self-harm in Aboriginal and Torres Strait Islander people', abs.gov.au/ausstats/abs@.nsf/Lookup/by%20Subject/3303.0~2015~Main%20Features~Intentional%20self-harm%20in%20Aboriginal%20and%20Torres%20Strait%20Islander%20people~9

LGBTQIA+ folk more than five times as likely to die by suicide: National LGBTI Health Alliance, 'Snapshot of mental health and suicide prevention statistics for LGBTI people, February 2020', d3n8a8pro7vhmx.cloudfront.net/lgbtihealth/pages/549/attachments/original/1595492235/2020-Snapshot_mental_health_%281%29.pdf?1595492235

Chapter 6: Seeking a Diagnosis

Out of fifty test subjects, thirty-nine were male: F.R. Volkmar, D.J. Cohen and R. Paul 'An evaluation of *DSM-III* criteria for infantile autism', *Child and Adolescent Psychiatry*, vol. 25, no. 2, March 1986, pp. 190–97, jaacap.org/article/S0002-7138(09)60226-0/fulltext

Six points of diagnostic criteria and symptoms evident before thirty months of age: *Diagnostic and Statistical Manual of Mental Disorders: Third Edition* (*DSM-III*), American Psychiatric Association/Cambridge University Press, Cambridge, 1975.

In 1987, the updated manual significantly altered the criteria: D.C. Factor, N.L. Freeman and A. Kardash, 'Brief report: A comparison of *DSM-III* and *DSM-III-R* criteria for autism', *Journal of Autism and Developmental Disorders*, vol. 19, December 1989, pp. 637–40, doi.org/10.1007/BF02212862

One in 160 people are autistic, many studies show as high as one in 50; 98 per cent of Australians have heard of autism, and 86 per cent know an autistic person: 'Autism fast facts', Amaze, amaze.org.au/wp-content/uploads/2019/06/General-Understanding-Fast-Facts.pdf

Autistic people are four times more likely to experience depression than other groups: C. Hudson, L. Hall and K. Harkness, 'Prevalence of depressive disorders in individual with autism spectrum disorder: A meta-analysis', *Journal*

of Abnormal Child Psychology, vol. 47, no. 1, January 2019, pp. 165–75, pubmed.ncbi.nlm.nih.gov/29497980/

Boys are four times more likely to be diagnosed than their female counterparts: R. McCrossin, 'Finding the true number of females with autistic spectrum disorder by estimating the biases in initial recognition and clinical diagnosis', *Children*, vol. 9, no. 2, 17 February 2022, p. 272, mdpi.com/2227-9067/9/2/272

Autistic people are four times more likely to experience depression, roughly 40 per cent of young autistic women have an anxiety disorder: F.J. van Steensel, S.M. Bogels and S. Perrin, 'Anxiety disorders in children and adolescents with autistic spectrum disorders: A meta-analysis', *Clinical Child and Family Psychology Review*, vol. 14, no. 3, 2011, pp. 302–17, doi:10.1007/s10567-011-0097-0; F.J.A. van Steensel and E.J. Heeman, 'Anxiety levels in children with autism spectrum disorder: A meta-analysis', *Journal of Child and Family Studies*, vol. 26, no. 7, March 2017, pp. 1753–67, doi:10.1007/s10826-017-0687-7

Insomnia affects 73 to 80 per cent of autistic people: S.E. Goldman, K. Surdyka, R. Cuevas et al., 'Defining the sleep phenotype in children with autism', *Developmental Neuropsychology*, vol. 34, no. 5, 2009, pp. 560–73, pubmed.ncbi.nlm.nih.gov/20183719/

Autistic people are thirteen times more likely to be diagnosed with OCD (6 per cent): S.M. Meier, L. Petersen, D.E. Schendel et al., 'Obssessive-compulsive disorder and autism spectrum disorders: Longitudinal and offspring risk', *PLos ONE*, vol. 10, no. 11, 2015, ncbi.nlm.nih.gov/pmc/articles/PMC4641696/

ADHD was described in the DSM-II *in one sentence*: *Diagnostic and Statistical Manual of Mental Disorders: Second Edition* (*DSM-II*), American Psychiatric Association, 1968.

Ten per cent of women with ADHD are diagnosed with depression, 38 per cent meet criteria for an anxiety disorder: I. Tung, J.J. Li, J.I. Meza et al., 'Patterns of comorbidity among girls with ADHD: A meta-analysis', *Pediatrics*, vol. 138, no. 4, 2016, publications.aap.org/pediatrics/article-abstract/138/4/e20160430/77134/Patterns-of-Comorbidity-Among-Girls-With-ADHD-A

Up to 99 per cent of people with ADHD are more sensitive to rejection, one in three say it's the most difficult part of being ADHD: S. Watson, 'What is rejection sensitive dysphoria?', WebMD, 13 September 2020, webmd.com/add-adhd/rejection-sensitive-dysphoria

More than 67 per cent of people with ADHD struggle with sleep issues: S. Bhandari, 'Adult ADHD and sleep problems', WebMD, 8 July 2021, webmd.com/add-adhd/adult-adhd-and-sleep-problems

Study shows Asperger assisted in the murder of disabled children: H. Czech, 'Hans Asperger, National Socialism, and "race hygiene" in Nazi-era Vienna', *Molecular Autism*, vol. 9, 2018, pp. 1–43, doi.org/10.1186/s13229-018-0208-6

Chapter 8: Eye Sparkles

Ninety-five per cent of the autistic population have what was called 'obsessions', intense special interests: L.M. Turner-Brown, K.S.L. Lam, T.N. Holtzclaw et al., 'Phenomenology and measurement of circumscribed interests in autism spectrum disorders', *Autism*, vol. 15, no. 4, July 2011, pp. 437–56, journals.sagepub.com/doi/10.1177/1362361310386507

Chapter 9: Adulting

Studies have shown autistic people who menstruate have higher rates of menstrual problems: H. Roy, A. Hergüner, S. Simsek et al., 'Autistic traits in women with primary dysmenorrhea: A case–control study', *Neuropsychiatic Disease and Treatment*, vol. 12, 2016, pp. 2319–25, ncbi.nlm.nih.gov/pmc/articles/PMC5026176/

Seventy-eight per cent of autistic women are sexually assaulted: 'Scope of the problem: Statistics', RAINN, rainn.org/statistics/scope-problem

Twenty per cent of autistic Australians have lost jobs due to being autistic: S. Jones, M. Akram, N. Murphy et al., 'Australia's attitudes and behaviours towards autism; and experiences of autistic people and their families', Autism and Education, Research Report for AMAZE, 26 September 2018, amaze.org.au/wp-content/uploads/2019/06/Education-Community-Attitudes-and-Lived-Experiences-Research-Report_FINAL.pdf

Women get paid an average of 16.8 per cent less than men: Workplace Gender Equality Agency, Australia's Gender Pay Gap Statistics, February 2022, wgea.gov.au/publications/australias-gender-pay-gap-statistics

Australia ranks lowest among OECD countries for income of disabled employees: M. Thomas, 'Disability employment in Australia and the OECD', Parliament of Australia, 2 December 2011, aph.gov.au/About_Parliament/Parliamentary_Departments/Parliamentary_Library/FlagPost/2011/December/Disability_employment_in_Australia_and_the_OECD

Some 31.6 per cent of autistic people are deemed unemployable: 'Autism and Employment in Australia', Amaze, amaze.org.au/creating-change/research/employment/

Sir Ken Robinson, 'Do schools kill creativity?', TEDx Talk, February 2006, ted.com/talks/sir_ken_robinson_do_schools_kill_creativity

Index